Policy Stability and Economic Growth

POLICY STABILITY AND ECONOMIC GROWTH

Lessons from the Great Recession

JOHN B. TAYLOR

with commentaries by

PATRICK MINFORD

ANDREW G. HALDANE AND AMAR RADIA

Institute of
Economic Affairs

First published in Great Britain in 2016 by
The Institute of Economic Affairs
2 Lord North Street
Westminster
London SW1P 3LB
in association with London Publishing Partnership Ltd
www.londonpublishingpartnership.co.uk

The mission of the Institute of Economic Affairs is to improve understanding
of the fundamental institutions of a free society by analysing and expounding
the role of markets in solving economic and social problems.

A CIP catalogue record for this book is available from the British Library.

ISBN 978-0-255-36719-6

Many IEA publications are translated into languages other
than English or are reprinted. Permission to translate or to reprint
should be sought from the Director General at the address above.

Typeset in Kepler by T&T Productions Ltd
www.tandtproductions.com

Printed and bound in Great Britain by Page Bros

CONTENTS

Andrew G. Haldane

Andrew G. Haldane is the Chief Economist at the Bank of England and Executive Director, Monetary Analysis and Statistics. He is a member of the Bank's Monetary Policy Committee. He also has responsibility for research and statistics across the Bank. In 2014, *Time* magazine named him one of the 100 most influential people in the world. Andrew has written extensively on domestic and international monetary and financial policy issues. He is co-founder of 'Pro Bono Economics', a charity which brokers economists into charitable projects.

Patrick Minford

Patrick Minford is Professor of Applied Economics at Cardiff University, where he directs the Julian Hodge Institute of Applied Macroeconomics. Between 1967 and 1976 he held a variety of economic positions, including spells in East Africa, in industry and at HM Treasury. From 1976 to 1997 he was the Edward Gonner Professor of Applied Economics at Liverpool University. He was a Member of the Monopolies and Mergers Commission from 1990 to 1996, and one of the HM Treasury's Panel of Forecasters (the 'Six Wise Men') from 1993 to 1996. He was made a CBE in 1996.

He has written widely on macroeconomics and related policy issues.

Amar Radia

Amar Radia is a manager in the Financial Stability Strategy and Risk Directorate at the Bank of England. He was previously an economist in the Bank's Monetary Analysis Directorate.

John B. Taylor

Professor John B. Taylor is the Robert Raymond Professor of Economics at Stanford University and the George P. Shultz Senior Fellow in Economics at the Hoover Institution. John Taylor's academic fields of expertise are macroeconomics, monetary economics and international economics. In particular, he is known for his research on the foundations of modern monetary theory and policy. He has served on the US President's Council of Economic Advisors, the US Congressional Budget Office's panel of Economic Advisors and the California Governor's Council of Economic Advisors. From 2001 to 2005, John Taylor was Under Secretary of the US Treasury for International Affairs, where he was responsible for, amongst other things, currency markets, trade in financial services and oversight of the International Monetary Fund and the World Bank.

FOREWORD

John Taylor is one of the world's foremost economists. He has not only bridged the divide between theory and policymaking; it can be argued that his contributions were important in promoting stability, higher levels of employment and an environment of low inflation over two decades in much of the Western world. He is one of relatively few economists whose work can be said to have had a profound effect for the good on policy.

In this short monograph, reproduced from his 2014 Hayek lecture, Taylor argues that deviating from strict policy rules, both before and since the crisis, contributed to the events of 2008–13 and, especially, the very slow recovery in national income after the financial crisis. Furthermore, in other areas of government activity, such as regulation and law-making more generally, instability is being created, which is very bad for the economy.

If we take the long view, in the UK there has been remarkable stability in prices. Indeed, stable prices were the norm in the UK until the mid twentieth century. There were certainly price spikes after, for example, crop failures or during wars. However, in general, these tended to be compensated by a general fall in prices at other times. Certainly, inflation, if this is understood to be a sustained, continuing rise in prices, was rare over any considerable time period. Overall, between 1750 and 1900, inflation averaged just 0.3 per cent per year. For much of this period, policy was anchored by the application of rules, such as a fixed price between gold and the domestic currency and free convertibility between the currency and gold.

The adherence to rules and institutional devices designed to ensure stable prices broke down after World War II. There were still constraints on government, such as the tying of exchange rates through the Bretton Woods system. However, such constraints, though better than nothing, were not very helpful when many of the countries that had their currencies tied to each other were following erratic monetary policy. By the time the dollar's tie to gold ended in 1971, a belief in discretionary policy had triumphed over rules and institutions.

Indeed, in reality, policy became so erratic before the break of the dollar from gold in 1971 that the break was inevitable and a symptom of monetary disorder, rather than a single event that caused policy to lose its anchor. Why did this happen? After World War II, policymakers became convinced that they could guide the economy with discretionary monetary and fiscal policy, 'stepping on the brakes' when the economy was overheating and 'putting a foot on the accelerator' when unemployment and output were likely to fall below trend. However, in reality, this increased instability: economists did not know as much as they believed they did about the underlying state of the economy and the effect of their policy actions. In addition, there was a strong asymmetric bias towards inflation.

Unfortunately, without an anchor for policy, governments found it very difficult to commit credibly to low inflation. Even if governments wished to promise low inflation, electorates would suspect that, if the going got tough, the central bank (under instruction) would loosen monetary policy to try to engineer a short-term rise in output and employment, especially if an election was round the corner. Political parties would not be rewarded at elections for promising monetary stability because there was no way of convincing the electorate that they would stick to their promises. In Britain in the 1970s, inflation averaged over 14 per cent a year, and employment and output performance were disappointing too.

Independent central banks following explicit targets and rules helped to resolve this credibility gap. The government set up the institutions or created a transparent framework, so it became much more difficult for the government to interfere. Inflation fell dramatically and, more generally, a number of Western countries had excellent growth and employment records. There was a long period of stability up to the point of the financial crash.

It is in the run-up to the financial crash that John Taylor's story about the break from rules starts. In a fascinating analysis, he describes how the Federal Reserve started using much more discretion, especially in the early 2000s. It continued in this way after the crisis of 2008. Ultimately, rules-based frameworks broke down in other areas too, and planning within the private sector became much more difficult: hence the sluggish response after the output slump following the financial crisis. John Taylor's message is that we must return to a situation where governments (together with surrounding institutions) follow rules rather than use their own discretion. More generally, governments should promote economic freedom rather than intervene in a discretionary way in the economy.

Two very interesting commentaries follow the Hayek lecture. The first, by Patrick Minford, suggests that a Taylor rule[1] that tried to keep inflation under control might not have been enough to avert the financial crisis, even if it had been followed. Professor Minford proposes a framework that involves targeting nominal national income instead – we should still follow rules, but the targets would be different.

Andrew Haldane and Amar Radia do not agree with John Taylor's analysis – at least not in its entirety. They argue that central banks should use discretion: discretion within constraints, but discretion nevertheless. This short book is rounded off with a brief response from John Taylor, who very succinctly restates the case for rules-based policy and addresses the critics.

Overall, this collection is timely and should be very helpful to students, teachers, policymakers and all those interested in economic policy debates. The debates surrounding monetary policy, so-called macro-prudential regulation and financial regulation are important. The out-turn of such debates will determine whether countries

---

1   A Taylor rule specifies by how much a central bank should change the nominal interest rate in response to a change in inflation or other macroeconomic variable. Adherence to such a rule can reduce uncertainty and thus improve an economy's performance.

can retain thriving financial sectors and have stable economies more generally. This collection is an important contribution to these debates. The Institute of Economic Affairs (IEA) would like to thank CQS for its sponsorship of the Hayek lecture, and Professor John Taylor for giving such a stimulating talk.

The views expressed in this monograph are, as in all IEA publications, those of the authors and not those of the Institute (which has no corporate view), its managing trustees, Academic Advisory Council members or senior staff. With some exceptions, such as with the publication of lectures such as this one, all IEA monographs are blind peer-reviewed by at least two academics or researchers who are experts in the field.

PHILIP BOOTH

Editorial and Programme Director
Institute of Economic Affairs
Professor of Finance, Public Policy and Ethics
St Mary's University, Twickenham

December 2015

ACKNOWLEDGEMENT

The IEA would like to thank CQS for its very generous sponsorship of the 2014 Hayek Memorial Lecture and of this publication.

SUMMARY

John Taylor's Hayek lecture

- The recovery from the recession after the financial crisis, in both the UK and the US, has been very slow compared with other similar events in history.
- During the period before the financial crash and afterwards, monetary policy deviated from the very effective rules-based approach of the previous two decades. In 2003–5, there was a huge gap between actual interest rates and the level suggested by the Taylor rule. This was at least partly responsible for the crash and the following slow recovery.
- Other areas of policy also became erratic. Unconventional monetary policy was followed and there were fiscal stimulus packages with changes in taxes and special subsidies offered to particular types of economic activity. In the US, there has been an enormous increase in the number of federal workers engaged in regulatory activity. Between 2006 and 2012, the number grew from around 180,000 to nearly 240,000 (excluding those employed in national security). In the 1980s, the reverse happened.
- In the 20 years or so before the run-up to the financial crash, there had been adherence to stable, rules-based

policy combined with good economic performance. In the period since, there has been more discretion, and bad results have followed. In order to return to success we need to ensure that 'the wind of freedom blows' (in the words of the motto of Stanford University).

Commentary by Patrick Minford

- Although it is true that monetary policy was too loose before the financial crash, it may be the case that adhering to a rule such as a Taylor rule, when combined with inflation targeting, is insufficient to deal with a build-up of liquidity in the financial sector. In an inflation-targeting regime, for various reasons, inflation might stay close to target even after a prolonged period of loose monetary policy. Thus, the central bank will take too little action too late.
- Rules are, nevertheless, important. A Taylor-type rule combined with a central bank target for nominal national income is likely to lead to greater monetary tightening more quickly as an expansion develops. It is, therefore, less likely to create financial instability. Indeed, model simulations suggest that financial crises would be very unusual in such a regime.

Commentary by Andrew Haldane and Amar Radia

- Even when rules are applied in policymaking, judgement has to be used too. For example, the application of a Taylor rule requires a judgement about the size of the output gap and the equilibrium level of interest rates at which monetary policy is neutral.

- In practice, most monetary policy regimes have settled on a system of 'constrained discretion'. This sets a framework within which decisions should be made while also allowing judgements to be made in the implementation of policy. In such systems, it is important that there are mechanisms that prevent natural biases from affecting policy unduly. For example, committee structures and the use of external members on the Bank of England's Monetary Policy Committee can reduce 'group-think bias'.
- The relatively new field (in the UK) of macro-prudential policy does not have a clear benchmark – such as the Taylor rule – against which it can easily be assessed. This may lead to time inconsistency and unpredictability. Over time, there may be scope for developing benchmark macro-prudential rules.

Rejoinder by John Taylor

- Rules promote accountability, especially because the results of monetary policy decisions work with long and variable lags, so that it is difficult to simply look at inflation and determine if policymakers are doing a good job. While there are problems that must be tackled when implementing monetary policy rules, these problems are not serious enough to override the many advantages of policy rules, nor, in the bigger picture, to override the more general advantages of predictable policies based on the rule of law and other key principles of economic freedom.

TABLES AND FIGURES

1 POLICY STABILITY AND ECONOMIC GROWTH: LESSONS FROM THE GREAT RECESSION

Introduction

It is particularly nice to be here at the Institute of Economic Affairs (IEA), which I have heard about, studied and looked to for many years. I have had a long interest in how economics is used in policy, the world of ideas and the world of government, and I think this institute has proven over the years how important ideas are for good government. I read, in thinking about this lecture, that the founder of the institute, Antony Fisher, first got the idea when he was a fighter pilot in World War II, flying for the Royal Air Force. He read in the *Readers' Digest* the condensed version of *The Road to Serfdom*. He said, 'These are some ideas that I want to promote', and, after the war, he did so and set up this institution. It is a very important institution, and I am happy to be here.

I also admire the IEA's focus on free markets and all the benefits that kind of philosophy gives to people. I like the stress on, if you like, non-partisan issues. Anyone who wants to listen to the benefits of free markets and a free society is welcome. That is what I think a good institution should be all about.

The Great Recession compared with earlier recessions

I want to focus on lessons learned from our experience over the last few years in the financial crisis and the slow recovery from the Great Recession, because I think it is tremendously important to figure out what went wrong and what we can do better in the future: the lessons to be learned.

To me, there is a striking similarity between my country, the US, and the UK in terms of what actually happened. What I am going to present are ideas that came to me from thinking about economic policies in the US and, actually, before that, from thinking about particular kinds of policies in the US – especially monetary policy, which is my expertise, if you like, or my love, and seeing how the problems with monetary policy actually extend to other kinds of policies. I think that these ideas are useful for thinking about the UK as well.

So, let me begin with a description of where we are in the US and in the UK. First, let's take a look at Figure 1. This is a chart of real GDP in the US, and you can see it goes back to before the crisis in 2007. The lower line shows real GDP, the total amount of goods and services produced in a given year in the US, adjusted for inflation. There is a big dip, that is the Great Recession with the financial crisis, and then there is recovery. I have superimposed on that the previous trend of real GDP from 2000 to 2007. You can see the recovery looks like a great disappointment. We have had a recovery in the sense that growth has generally proceeded at a positive rate. Why is it disappointing? It is

Figure 1   Great Recession and not-so-great recovery (US)

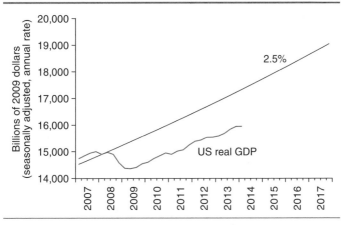

disappointing because we did not bounce back as we have in previous recoveries.

Now, what about the UK? Let us look at the same kind of chart for the UK, at the behaviour of real GDP since 2007 (Figure 2), before the Great Recession, and then at the recovery, and superimpose on that the trend line from 2000 through 2007.

You can see that the path of real GDP is quite similar to the US but worse, because it is even slower than the trend line before. So, in both of these cases, there has been a disappointing lack of recovery.

One way to think about these recoveries is to compare them with the recoveries from the previous, most recent deep recessions. Focus on the US first. A deep recession took place in the early 1980s. In Figure 3, you can see that real GDP declines, but then it bounces back. If we had seen

Figure 2 Great Recession and not-so-great recovery (UK)

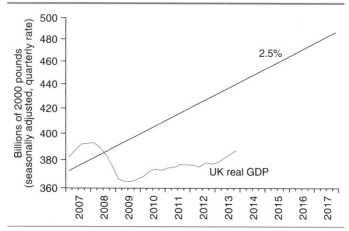

this kind of recovery this time, we would already be back producing many more trillions of dollars a year.

That is a typical recovery. The same thing is true for the UK. If you look at that same time period in the UK (Figure 4), the bounce-back from recession is much better. This is what should happen in a typical recovery.

So, we had not only this very deep recession, but also this poor recovery: the 'Great Recession' and the 'not-so-great recovery'. The questions are: why the deep recession and why the slow recovery?

I think the answers to both questions are related. The same kinds of things have affected both the recession and then the recovery.

Other people, of course, have different views, and I want to touch on those briefly. One view is this: 'What do you

Figure 3 US recession and recovery in early 1980s

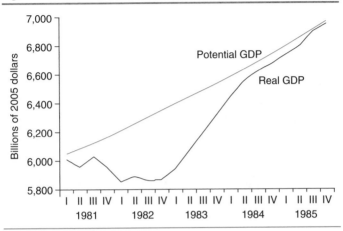

expect? We had this deep recession. The economy is not going to bounce back that fast.' However, the charts comparing previous recoveries in the US and UK illustrate that is not the case. Figure 5 provides more evidence. It shows the speed of recovery for all of the deep recessions associated with a financial crisis in the US going back to the 1880s. The top horizontal line is the average growth rate in the first two years of all of those recoveries: the average is about 6 per cent. The lower line shows the growth rate during the recovery after the recent financial crisis: this was about 2 per cent. This is easily the worst recovery after a financial crisis.

So, it really is not correct to say that recent experience is what you would expect from a financial crisis: something else is going on.

Figure 4   UK recession and recovery in early 1980s

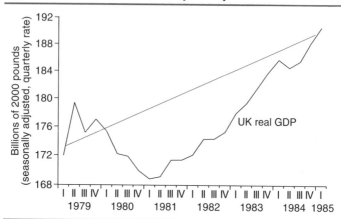

There are other explanations. One theory that has been offered more recently runs as follows: the income distribution has spread and widened, and this leads to slower growth because people at the lower end of the income distribution consume more as a fraction of their income than those at the top, and they are getting relatively less than before. It is argued that this leads to less consumption and less growth.

But this does not fit the data either. The fast US recovery in the 1980s was during a period when saving rates were higher than they have been recently.

The principles of good policy

So, there are various possibilities that people have offered for this experience, but the conclusion that I have come to is that there has been a problem with policy, and that

Figure 5   Growth rate in first eight quarters of a recovery from previous recessions with a financial crisis (identified by year recession began)

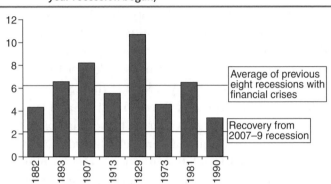

policy is really the key to understanding what went wrong both leading up to the crisis and since the crisis.

So, what is good policy?

The first principle of good policy is that we should have a situation where families, entrepreneurs and everyone else are free to make decisions within a *clear policy framework that is predictable*, so you know what is going on, what the government is going to do, and you have some sense of the future. Secondly, policy should be based on a *strong rule of law*. Thirdly, there should be *strong incentives* for people to do things that improve their own welfare, and the welfare of society. Fourth, those incentives should largely come from the *free-market system*.

Of course, there is a role for government, and this is the fifth principle: that this *role for government should be limited* in the sense that the government's role is based on some reasonable cost-benefit analysis. When the cost-benefit analysis indicates that the government should do it, that's fine. Otherwise, the private sector should do it.

What I have observed in thinking about recent events is that we sometimes adhere to these principles of good policy more closely, and sometimes we deviate from them.

First, consider the US. As I look at the US, I see these shifting winds of economic freedom. In the late 1960s and 1970s, we were shifting away from these principles. Monetary policy became quite unpredictable and was known as 'go-stop'. It led to a lot of inflation and a lot of unemployment. Fiscal policy was quite erratic. We had a lot of Keynesian stimulus packages. This was true under both parties: Republicans and Democrats.

We had wage and price controls for the entire economy. How is that for trying to avoid the market system? We had a large increase in the number of regulations during that period, and a large increase in the scope of government.

I come to this from the monetary-policy side, and that is where I see these shifts in policy most of all.

Performance was not very good during this period; we had high inflation and high unemployment in the US. What about the UK? Some of you remember what it was like. It was not so good in the 1970s. You had high inflation, high unemployment and a lot of problems. I think that, if you look at the policies, you will see similarities. They're not exactly the same, but monetary policy and fiscal policy had the same sort of problems that I have described in the US.

Then, we saw a change. Again, I am first thinking about the US. We saw a change in policy. Monetary policy became more predictable: less go-stop, more rule-like. I'll come back to that in a minute. Fiscal policy moved away from the Keynesian stimulus packages. It basically tried to get the tax system right and not change it too much. We made a huge effort in this time to reduce the amount of regulations.

The change began in the late 1970s, and it continued in the 1980s. Ronald Reagan became president and Paul Volcker was appointed Chairman of the Federal Reserve by Reagan's predecessor, Jimmy Carter: a democrat.

So, there was a change. What happened? Performance was remarkably good during this period. Economists call this the 'Great Moderation'.

The UK was not too dissimilar. There was a change in policy. Think about how monetary policy began to change. Think about how fiscal policy began to change. Think about how trade union policy began to change.

Then, finally, during this more recent period, there has been a veering away from these principles. Here, I am thinking mainly about my country. In the US, I saw monetary policy in 2003, 2004 and 2005 hold interest rates too low for too long. This was a deviation from the more predictable policy of the 1980s and 1990s. Fiscal policy again became more short-term Keynesian, which it tends to be to this day. Regulation increased – I will talk more about that in a minute.

Now, what about the UK? Here, it seems to me, there is more research to be done, but there is a similarity: certainly with respect to monetary policy, and also with respect to other kinds of policies, including regulatory policy.

This is an important story to understand more fully, for what it suggests is that we should go back, in some sense, to the kind of policy that emphasised markets more, emphasised the rule of law and emphasised the predictability of policies with a limited role for government.

Monetary policy: to the Taylor rule and back

So, given that background, now let me give you some details to fill in the blanks of these broad, even gross, generalisations. I want to spend most of my time on monetary policy, which is my favourite area of study. I am going to first illustrate these changes with some simple graphs.

Figure 6 shows the inflation rate in the US going back to the mid 1950s. You can see how it increased and decreased. The great inflation period was the bad period, and then it got better.

Figure 6   Inflation from 1953 to 2013

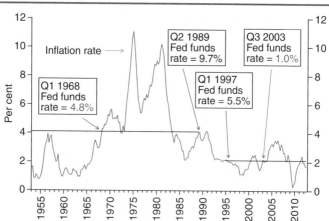

Monetary policy is also indicated on the same chart, along with several snapshots of interest rate levels set by the Federal Reserve (Fed).

In Figure 6, there is also a horizontal line drawn at an inflation rate of 4 per cent. In 1968, the interest rate (federal funds rate) was 4.8 per cent, just a smidgeon above the inflation rate: not really enough to contain the inflation, not enough to put downward pressure on inflation and not enough of a tightening of policy to lead to price stability. Lo and behold, inflation rose and continued to rise until there was a change.

Then, if you look following the change in the policy environment, you can see the same inflation rate, 4 per cent, and the federal funds rate was almost twice as high at 9.7 per cent. That was quite a different policy.

The shift in policy involved a move from a stop-go stimulative type of policy, which backfired, to one that was more sensible, focused on price stability, and the inflation rate was much lower. In addition, the unemployment rate came down. Now, if we continue this line of argument, we can see the veering away from good policy. I have drawn a line in Figure 6 at an inflation rate of 2 per cent and, again, note two interest rate decisions of the Federal Reserve. The first one was in 1997, when the interest rate was 5.5 per cent. That is the kind of interest rate that would tend to contain things: prevent inflation from rising, or prevent overheating or a search for yield or uncertainty. Then, see what was decided in 2003: the same inflation rate, roughly the same state of the economy, about the same level of capacity utilisation, and the interest rate is only 1 per cent.

This is a different policy, and this is the kind of change I am talking about. There is a shift in policy that you can see, I think, very clearly. Now, fortunately, there is more information to go on than just looking at these examples. What there is to go on is actually sometimes related to the so-called Taylor rule. Now, I have a problem. I wish it wasn't called the Taylor rule, because every time I mention it, I lose all credibility. Nobody believes what I say. People say: 'Well, the guy's just trying to promote his own rule.'

So, I am going to refer to other people's research on the rule. This will be more objective. Figure 7 shows actual policy as indicated by the federal funds rate from 1965 to 1995 in the solid line, and policy as suggested by a Taylor rule[1] using the dashed line.

This uses a picture actually produced by the Federal Reserve in 1995.

It can be seen that the interest rate was volatile in the 1960s and 1970s, but generally quite a bit below the Taylor rule. Then, you see the change I mentioned, with Paul Volcker coming in and Alan Greenspan replacing him. You see quite a bit of change. Now, we are going to the so-called good period I'm talking about, where policy is more rule-like, and you can see a surprising (to many people) correspondence between performance and this rules-based measure. During the last part of the period, there is an especially close correspondence.

So, that is a description of moving from a go-stop, non-rule-like policy to a rule-like policy. Then, look what

---

1   The rule used here is shown within the dashed ellipse.

Figure 7 1965–80: monetary policy not well described by good rules-based policy

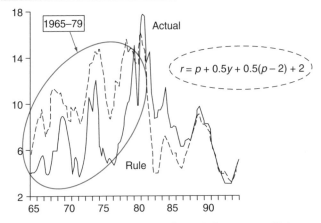

Source: 'Has the Fed Gotten Tougher on Inflation?' *The FRBSF Weekly Letter*, 31 March 1995, by John P Judd and Bharat Trehan of the Federal Reserve Bank of San Francisco.

happened. We have a period in 2003–5 when the interest rate gets very low. The Taylor rule guideline says it shouldn't be so low, and there is this gap. People began to write about it at the time. Figure 8 is a picture from *The Economist* magazine back in 2007. Its writers wrote in the term 'Taylor rule', not me, so I'm still maintaining some objectivity. You can see the gap between the actual interest rate and the Taylor rule. It is a huge gap.

So, that is the context. If you look at research and you look at the analysis, you can see that there was a change in

Figure 8   Loose-fitting monetary policy

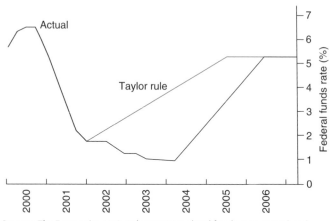

Source: *The Economist*, 18 October 2007. Federal funds rate, actual and counterfactual (in per cent).

the policy environment. The harm from this, of course, is that very low interest rates can cause a boom in the housing market, which I think they did. They can cause a search for yield and extra risk-taking, which I also think they did. Low interest rates may also have had something to do with regulators looking away when they saw extra risk-taking in commercial banks and other financial institutions. In any case, that seemed to happen at the same time.

So, these issues are important, and that is why I argue that part of the explanation for what happened is this deviation from rules-based policy and, in this case, from a simple policy rule.

Just to show you that this is not only relevant to the US (and before I come back to the UK), take a look at Figure 9, which was drawn up by the Organisation for Economic Co-operation and Development (OECD). It shows some of the striking international impact of deviations from the Taylor rule.

Figure 9   Housing investment versus deviations from the Taylor rule in the euro zone countries, 2001–6

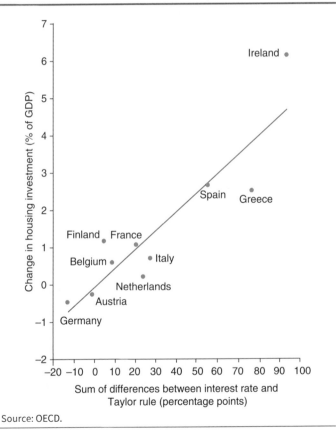

Source: OECD.

What Figure 9 tries to do is accumulate all of those gaps between the interest rate and the rule (that is, between non-rule-like and rule-like policy). It accumulates those gaps over a period of time from 2001 to 2006 (horizontal axis), and, on the vertical axis, it shows you how much of a housing boom there was in these countries. These countries are all in the euro zone, so the UK is not here. With only one interest rate for those countries, some are going to be closer to the rule and some are going to be further away. If you look at the ones that are further away (Ireland, Spain and Greece), you can see the effect. Those countries are away from the rule because the rates for those countries were too low at the time, and that added to the bubble-like behaviour that eventually led to the problems in those countries.

Now, what about the UK? The UK did not have an interest rate of 1 per cent, as you know, during that period of time. So, can you make the same argument?

Here, I want to refer to some work that the former Deputy Governor of the Bank of England, Charles Bean, performed back in 2010 (Bean et al. 2010). He found that the interest rate at the Bank of England was also too low in the years before the crisis, or below the level suggested by policy rules. He also found, and, to be sure, it is just one study and just an example, that 46 per cent of the housing boom price bubble observed in the UK was due to this policy.

So, there is some indication that something similar happened in the UK. I did not think about that at the time, when I first wrote about the US, but the problem seems to be there, as the other evidence shows, internationally as well.

Very unruly policy

Now, during the crisis, during the panic, during October and November 2008 especially, there were a lot of interventions by central banks. I would say they were good interventions, by the Bank of England and by the Fed and others, to stem the tide of panic: essentially, 'lender of last resort' activity.

So, in this period, even though I think the panic was due to a lot of the mistaken policies, a policy reaction to the panic came through that was quite good. But what happened after that? This is part of the question of why the recovery has been so weak.

Policies then went back to very unrule-like policies: unconventional, unprecedented kinds of policies. Quantitative easing in the US, forward guidance in the US, and all this at the Bank of England too.

There is debate about whether these actions worked. As I look at the analysis, I don't think they worked much at all. I think they did some harm. At the very least, they were not very rule-like or predictable: they had to change all the time.

Quantitative easing is very hard to describe in terms of some kind of a predictable procedure, so we deviated from rules, and I think that has continued to this day. There is a lot of talk about moving back to a more rules-based policy, but we are certainly not there yet. I put these post-crash policies forward as an example of this major shift from rule-like good policy and principles of economic freedom. Of course, the results were not so good.

There is a real question, of course, about going from correlation to causation, but let me just make a couple of observations about that.

The change in policy that took us from the bad 1970s to the better 1980s and 1990s occurred before the change in performance. There is no question about that. So, there is a lag from which you can identify the temporal causation. What about the move away from rules-based policy? Is it not unreasonable to say: 'Oh, they had to do all those things because of the financial crisis'? The truth is that many of these actions began before the financial crisis, and I am referring in particular to the Fed and, with some additional evidence, to the Bank of England and the other central banks that I discussed earlier. So, there is temporal causation there, too. Maybe there is room for debate, but I think it is quite clear.

Now, let me just mention some of the other areas in which we have moved away from rules-based policy. Firstly, there is fiscal policy. In the US, we moved back towards stimulus packages in 2008. This is not a partisan position: in 2008, President Bush had a stimulus package.

Let me illustrate the stimulus package (see Figure 10). Bush's stimulus package was not unlike Alistair Darling's stimulus package in the UK, in the sense that taxes were temporarily cut or money was handed to people. The top line shows disposable personal income for all Americans aggregated. There are two big blips. One was the 2008 stimulus, and the next was the 2009 stimulus. Below is actual consumption, again aggregated across all people in the US. You are really hard pushed to see that the 'stimulus' package stimulated consumption and thereby stimulated the economy.

Figure 10 Did the fiscal stimulus stimulate consumption?

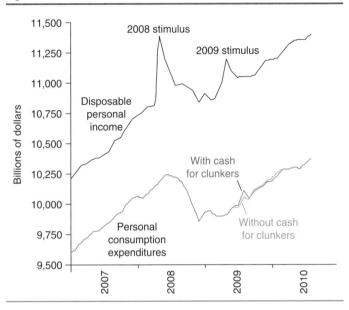

There is a further element that is very hard to see. Within the overall stimulus, there was a particular stimulus called 'cash for clunkers', where the government gave some payments to people who turned in their cars to buy new cars. This did not seem to have much of an effect at all. Any effect it had wore away after a little bit.

So, there is a lot of research like this that I've done and others have done, which, I think, raises questions about those policies. I don't want to say there is a consensus about this, and, indeed, there is quite a bit of debate, but I think this kind of chart tells you something important.

Figure 11 Debt to GDP ratio in the US

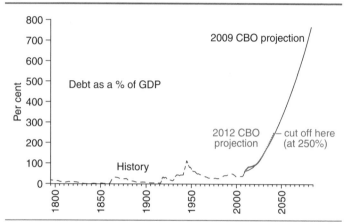

In any case, there was a return to the more discretionary, less rule-like fiscal policy that we used in the 1970s.

To some extent, the same thing happened in the UK. There was a temporary reduction of the value added tax. Did that have much of an effect? Well, you can tell me more than I can tell you from looking at the data, but it was temporary and had to be removed. It did not cause a sustainable expansion. There was a big increase in borrowing and a lot of increase in debt. This was not all because of policy, but some was, and that had to be reversed.

Indeed, the fiscal stimulus is a temporary thing. You maybe get something in the short run, but it falls away and so you do not have the sustained expansion that you really need to have. So, that's fiscal policy, and I could talk more about it, but I think you get the point.

Debt in the US as a share of GDP is on an unsustainable path, and policy has led to this. Figure 11 shows the ratio of our debt to GDP. It goes back to the beginning of the US. It is pretty low for most of the time, but there has been an explosion recently, and this has been projected by the Congressional Budget Office to continue. So, that is the debt legacy. This is not entirely due to the recent stimulus policies; to some extent, it is due to a more general lack of control on federal spending in the US.

The same thing, of course, is true for the UK, and that is why there has been an effort to address it.

Regulatory policy in the US is very similar. There has been a huge increase in the number of federal workers who are engaged in regulatory activity. Between 2006 and 2012, the number grew from around 180,000 to near-ly 240,000 (excluding Transport Security Administration (TSA) employees). That is a steady increase over a long period of time. If you look at the 1980s, there was the re-verse pattern. You have a decline in the number of people employed in regulation. The employment of regulators is just one part of the story. There are also new regulatory activities through the Dodd–Frank Act and a major change in healthcare regulation through the Affordable Care Act, sometimes called 'Obamacare'. So, there's a lot there.

It seems to me when you add all of this up – monetary policy, fiscal policy and regulation, and also taxation, which I have not discussed much – there are similar trends across countries. It is not exactly the same in each coun-try. Countries are different, with different timings and different issues, but I think there is a remarkable similarity that needs to be discussed.

A return to rules-based policy

The implication of all of this, it seems to me, is that we need to get back to the kinds of policies that worked well. I think we can learn a lot from Hayek when we do that. These principles are not at all unlike those Hayek wrote about. Let me just give you some examples.

The first two items on my list are predictable policy and the rule of law. They have not been stressed very much in economics over the years. Hayek emphasised them a lot. I listed them at the top because I know they are not stressed enough, and I wanted to put emphasis on them.

So, I have a little quote from *The Road to Serfdom*. It is a very good observation:

> Nothing distinguishes more clearly conditions in a free country from those in a country under arbitrary government than the observance in the former of the great principles known as the Rule of Law. Stripped of all technicalities, this means that government in all its actions is bound by rules fixed and announced beforehand – rules which make it possible to foresee with fair certainty how the authority will use its coercive powers in given circumstances and to plan one's individual affairs on the basis of this knowledge.

So, that is an important lesson. I think it comes partially from these observations from many years ago from Hayek, but I think we now know more about how important they are.

The second thing I would mention is that, in most of Hayek's writings, with which I am familiar, the stress on the rule of law is dual purpose. The way I have always thought about policy predictability and the rule of law is that it leads to better economic performance. Again, there are a lot of reasons for that, but it leads to more successful economies. Hayek emphasised another important benefit of rules, and that is that rules or laws protect individual freedom. In fact, that was a major focus of his *The Constitution of Liberty*.

Hayek referred to Cicero, saying that: 'No other author shows more clearly ... that freedom is dependent upon certain attributes of the law, its generality and certainty, and the restrictions it places on the discretion of authority'. Here is a quote from John Locke that appears in Hayek's writings: 'The end', by which he means the purpose, 'of the law is not to abolish or restrain, but to preserve and enlarge freedom. If there is no law, there is no freedom.'

So, this dual purpose, it seems to me, is an important lesson because it emphasises two good things about predictable policy and the rule of law. It leads to better performance, but it also leads to freedom in the broadest dimensions.

When you think about a policy rule, it does not mean that you don't do anything. I think it is important to emphasise that when we talk about 'rules-based policies' and 'predictable policy', it does not mean doing nothing. Hayek wrote about this very clearly. A monetary policy rule does not mean that you never change the interest rate. It means you change it in a predictable way that people can understand. It is quite movable; you are doing something. Think about law enforcement. Law enforcement does not mean you don't do anything. You go out, and you enforce the law. It takes a lot of action. It takes police on the street and it takes the court system.

The other thing we frequently say is that: 'It was a crisis. We had to do something different. We had to break the rules.' But my observation, from studying economics, is that a crisis is the worst time to break the rules, because there is so much else going on, and you need to keep some steadiness in policy.

Another lesson from Hayek is about who gets us in and out of these messes. I put a chapter about this in my recent book (Taylor 2012). As an academic researcher, I tend not to think about personalities so much as about policies. So, I have been talking about monetary policy and the rules monetary policy should follow, without mentioning people much. But, the truth is that people put these policies in place. Hayek wrote a lot about this. He had a chapter in *The Road to Serfdom* called 'Why the Worst Get on Top'. There's a tendency to be biased against strongly principled people: at least, that is my observation. Somehow, we need to deal with this.

One thought is that, when you are choosing people, you should look for those who are overly committed to the principles of economic freedom, as they will stay the course. Let's think of two examples.

President Reagan, when he came into office, was very principled. He actually had many advisers who were equally principled. Many of them had PhDs from the so-called Chicago School or related schools. This was really quite a bit of change from his predecessor's group of advisers. Reagan was certainly criticised for being committed, and, of course, Margaret Thatcher was too. There is a famous story that I like to tell, which you probably all know very well, that when she became leader of the Conservatives, she went to visit the research arm of the Conservative Party, called the Conservative Research Department, to see what was going on. One of the staffers made a presentation to her about looking for the middle way. Thatcher was infuriated; she looked into her handbag and just happened to have a copy of *The Constitution of Liberty*. It's a pretty big book. She pulled it out of her handbag, slammed it on the table, and said: 'This is what we're about. This is what we believe.'

However, these are the exceptions; the tendency is not to have such people in government, and that is why it is especially important that you have rules. Interestingly, Keynes had quite a different view of people, and he argued in reviewing and writing to Hayek about *The Road to Serfdom* that Hayek had it all wrong, and that all we need is good people and it will be fine: you only need to get the right people and it's going to be fine.

Finally, you have got to be steadfast. Even in the best of circumstances, there are going to be temptations for people to deviate from these principles. In fact, I have an example from Hayek himself. I think that in the 1970s he seemed to say that we had to have discretion in monetary policy. It was a period of discretionary monetary policy, and, like many people, he threw up his hands and said: 'What are we going to do?'

Milton Friedman objected to this view and wrote a letter to Hayek about it. In that letter, he said: 'I hate to see you come out as you do here for what I believe to be one of the most fundamental violations of the rule of law that we have, namely discretionary activities of central bankers'. It just shows you how hard it is sometimes to stick to the principles that I am talking about in tough times.

So, in conclusion, it's all pretty straightforward. If you look at the Great Recession and the period going into it, you can see deviations from good policy, and bad results followed. If you look at the period 20–25 years before that, you see adherence to good policy, and pretty good performance was the result. Then, if you look at the period before that, there was bad policy, and bad results followed.

Since I am a teacher from Stanford University, I am going to end by referring to Stanford University's seal. This is how I like to finish my course in elementary economics. Believe it or not, Stanford's unofficial motto is 'Die Luft der Freiheit weht', which is 'The Wind of Freedom Blows'.

For me, we have got to let the winds of economic freedom blow.

References

Bean, C., Paustian, M., Penalver, A. and Taylor, T. 2010 Monetary policy after the fall. https://www.kansascityfed.org/publicat/sympos/2010/Bean_final.pdf

Taylor, J. B. (2012) *First Principles: Five Keys to Restoring America's Prosperity.* New York: W. W. Norton.

2   QUESTIONS AND DISCUSSION

PHILIP BALL: I would like to know how you would reconcile your argument with the current debate on the rebalancing of the economy in terms of bringing back manufacturing to the UK. While I agree the period you referenced was very good in terms of the economy and it drove pharmaceuticals, for example, when it comes to other parts of manufacturing, it had a detrimental effect.

PROFESSOR TAYLOR: Yes, so the question is: 'What do you do about certain sectors such as manufacturing, especially with international competition?' First of all, I want to emphasise that what I have said here does not mean that good policy will make everything perfect. We have lots of other issues. It is a broad painting and a broad picture. In particular, if you think about some of the problems manufacturing has, at least in the US, they are frequently to do with regulation. There is an even broader set of issues about education, because a lot of the problems with manufacturing come down to the skills of the workers. How can you compete globally with a not-very-skilled workforce? This is not the topic of this talk, but I think a lot of the same things I mentioned in this talk could also be applied to education. In a way, economic freedom, as I emphasised here, if it is not provided equally, if you do not have equal opportunity, then you are going to make a mess. I think one of the problems, and again I am speaking about my own country, is that we have not provided equal opportunity to lots of people, and that has made education worse than it otherwise would be. I think that if you apply these principles more broadly, that could involve the use of the private sector and charter schools or vouchers. That could make a difference.

ROGER KENDRICK: Given the principles of economics and policy that you have explained this evening, do you think that we would have a more stable and prosperous economy inside or outside the European Union (EU), particularly if the euro zone is going to integrate further?

PROFESSOR TAYLOR: So, there is the EU and there is the euro zone. I think the EU is, to me, an opportunity to reduce barriers of all kinds. That is a benefit. I don't think there is much question about it. Again, let me refer to the US. We don't have a union. We have a free trade area with Canada, Mexico and the US. It has been very important for improving the economy and improving people's lives. I would not want to go back on that or somehow have the US drop out of that free trade area. There is one interesting difference though. We don't really have a central institution for the North American Free Trade Agreement. There is not a bureaucracy that runs it. So, that is a little different, and maybe the way to think about reform is to deal with that bureaucracy associated with the EU. I think it is an important difference, and we will see some differences in behaviour.

With respect to the euro zone and the European Central Bank (ECB), at this point I can't imagine that the UK would want to get involved in that. It seems to me that you have the opportunity to have a better policy than you have had recently. Joining the euro zone is not the way to go at this point, if that is what you are asking.

CYRIL TAYLOR: The US government is finding it difficult to sell its bonds when the interest rate is just 1 per cent, and, as I understand it, they are printing billions and billions of dollars. Would you agree that, eventually, this is going to increase inflation: if money is being printed rather than being earned by the production of goods?

PROFESSOR TAYLOR: Yes. I would agree with that. If there is not some effort to undo it or to move back to another kind of policy, there is definitely a huge risk of inflation. I think that policy has always had a two-sided risk, though. One is inflation, if it is not removed in time, and the other is if it causes uncertainty about the removal and what is going to happen. I think we have actually experienced that downside. It has really not helped. I cannot prove that it has been harmful, but I can prove that it has not done much good. My gut feeling is that the policy is harmful. The reason is that markets work best when there are a lot of participants and you are trying to figure out what is happening in the market in the usual way. So, when there is one huge player in the market, it works much differently, and I think it is very hard to discover prices. It is almost like wage and price control, though I understand that it is not the same thing.

The short-term money market in the US is basically completely ineffectual, because we have so much of a supply of liquidity out there that the rate is driven down effectively to zero, and the only way it can be moved is if the government pays the banks interest on reserves. So, that is a different kind of policy: that is not a market-based interest rate.

Those are things that concern me, but I would not put the inflation risks aside. We have had a disappointing economy. It has been weak. That has tended to make pressures on inflation less than they otherwise would be, but you can see signs of it. You never can tell exactly when it will pick up or where it will pick up. Sometimes, it does so gradually. That is how the great inflation came, at least in the US. It built up in the mid 1960s and 1970s, and suddenly we had this big inflation.

So, it could happen that way, but, hopefully, central banks will be able to remove the excess. There is a lot more talk about doing so recently than there was a year ago, so we could be hopeful.

JULIAN MORRIS: You made a very persuasive case in favour of rule-based monetary policy – a Taylor rule-based monetary policy. Unfortunately, governments around the world, including in the US and the UK, frequently see benefits in deviating from rule-based monetary policies, with monetising debt being one of the prime benefits in their view.

Is there an argument in favour of something even stricter than the Taylor rules commonly used? Hayek argued that money should be denationalised and we should perhaps move back towards a gold standard or some other system for creating a completely inflexible money supply. We now have the example of Bitcoin as one possible alternative. What is your view on these sorts of things?

PROFESSOR TAYLOR: My view, internationally, is that we are pretty close to something that has good characteristics, with some kind of stable price rule that I think is more flexible and workable. So, think about the following, and it is not just the Taylor rule in that context. There is an agreement between the Bank of Japan, the US, the Bank of England and even the ECB that the inflation target should be 2 per cent. That is what is in the Taylor rule. There is also a growing sense that you have to examine what the equilibrium short-term interest rate is. It is estimated to be about 4 per cent in the US by the Federal Reserve, or close to that. That is also in the policy rule. There is a huge amount of agreement about how much the interest rate should react when inflation picks up. So, my sense is that you are getting close to something that works internationally. Again, since there is always an ability to move away from it, it may not be as stable as you would like, but there was an ability to move off the gold standard too. What I am recommending, and I am not sure it is going to go anywhere right now, is that in the US we pass some legislation that requires the Fed to follow a policy rule. It would not be my rule; it would be the Fed's rule. It would be what they decide: that is, it would be their job to decide the rule, but, if they deviated from it, they would have to come and explain to Congress and the American people the reasons. Again, having looked at the history for a while, it seems to me that it is reasonable to try to do that. I think the Fed would resist that, but, ultimately, I think they would be able to work with it quite well.

BRONWYN CURTIS: You didn't talk or say anything about the structural changes that took place in the world during that period of the 1960s and 1970s. You had the opening up of trade through the General Agreement on Tariffs and Trade (GATT) and all of that, but when we get into the 1980s and particularly into the 1990s, of course, we have the opening up of China, the impact of much lower product prices and imported inflation coming into the Western world generally. Do you think that policymakers, particularly central bankers, may have confused the signals that they were looking at, so that they started to change the rules as we came in the 2000s? As you say, you didn't really talk about why they changed the rules.

PROFESSOR TAYLOR: I don't think that was the problem, at least with the policymakers I talked to. They may have said, 'Hey, we're getting a little help from globalisation' or things like that. But you can have high inflation in a globalised economy, and you can have low inflation in a globalised economy. It is really monetary policy that is determining inflation.

In terms of what went wrong, I don't know all of the reasons. I have good friends in the Federal Reserve. Alan Greenspan is a close friend. I think a lot of it was a 'perfect is the enemy of the good' problem; things were doing pretty well for a long time, and they wanted to do even better. As I look at the thinking, it was more like that: 'Let's get rates a little lower. It is going to help against the threat of deflation.' But it had unintended consequences. So, I think it is more like that, but the political economy of this is very important. I agree.

IVAN ATANASOFF: I met with my financial adviser ten days ago, and he said I was very overexposed to North America and should leave him to come up with another solution. Having reflected overnight, I thought that the affordable energy that was being produced through fracking would help America's economy to continue. Am I right in thinking this?

PROFESSOR TAYLOR: Energy is an area that I have focused on a lot. It is one of those things that makes you optimistic about the future, as technology is really promising and fracking is part of that. I think you obviously have to think about the environmental aspects of it, but, right now, my observation is that it is a huge benefit. We are too concerned about the regulation of it. It is an example of the reasons why you have to be optimistic. If we can get our act together on the policy issues, then we won't have these terrible slow-growth recoveries.

BARRY MACLENNAN: I am interested in looking at how the quantitative easing unwinds in the end, because your charts were showing very low interest rates and how expansion was going on quite dramatically. There would seem to be a huge pent-up problem in quantitative easing (QE), as the rules have to be made more fixed, known and so forth. Could you say a little bit more about that, particularly also about the economics of it?

PROFESSOR TAYLOR: The main concern I have had about QE since it began in 2009 in the US – and, again, I'm not talking about the actions during the panic (it is after that) – has been unwinding. It was originally a very huge increase in the quantity of money. It has got higher and higher and higher. So, the unwinding is a concern, because if it is not done fast enough, then you have this inflationary potential that I was just asked about. If it is unwound too quickly, it could have other undesirable impacts. People don't know the impact of these things. A lot of people think the stock market is doing well just because of QE. I don't agree with that, but if enough people think this is the case, then QE is going to have some detrimental effects on the market when it is unwound. So, it is tricky. Plus, at the same time, they will have to be raising interest rates.

Central bankers are deliberating about this as we speak. In the US, they will, for sure, raise the interest rate by increasing interest on reserves, as least for a while: at least until the balance sheet gets down, so you get supply closer to the demand for reserves.

To me, there is a danger that this situation will become permanent, that they will just leave the balance sheet high and use it for more interventions, and that they will set the interest rate based on paying interest on reserves. I think they are still trying to figure that out themselves. But, in the meantime, you have just the kind of thing that our guest is worried about. You had an example of it last year with the so-called taper tantrum, where just talking about the removal of QE caused a lot of turbulence. However, this more recent tapering, as we call it, has been more successful, I think, because it is clear: it is a strategy. You might not like it, but it is a strategy, and markets have been able to adapt to it well. So, that, to me, is a lesson on how you could unwind. You have a strategy, if you like, to sell a certain amount of securities month-by-month or quarter-by-quarter, and if people understand what the strategy is, I don't think it would have a detrimental effect at all.

That would be what I would recommend.

JOHN EATWELL: The Chancellor of the Exchequer has characterised British economic policy as, if you like, a trade-off between fiscal austerity, which makes space, it is argued, for a loose monetary policy. In the context of your rule-based monetary policy, that concept of a trade-off does not seem to be valid. Is that correct?

PROFESSOR TAYLOR: It is correct in the sense that you choose a rule and you stick to that. If the fiscal authorities do something that is crazy, you stick to your rule. If they say,

'I'm sorry, we can't stimulate the economy. You stimulate it', you stick to your rule. Now, there can be impacts of those bad policies on the economy or on inflation, which you will then react to, but, for the most part, I think the real big lesson we are learning from this is that monetary policy should stick to its business. Many central bankers I talk to don't like the situation they're in. They say: 'We were forced to do this. The government wouldn't do anything. We had to do it.' That is certainly a line we frequently hear. So, I think it is one of these situations. If a government agency says 'we will do this', people are going to ask them to do it, and they'll end up doing it. If it doesn't, the people who should be doing it, the fiscal authorities, will do it.

3 WAS FAILURE TO FOLLOW THE TAYLOR RULE ENOUGH TO CAUSE THE CRISIS?

A commentary on John Taylor's lecture

Patrick Minford

John Taylor has made substantial contributions to macro-economic theory and applied work as well as to policy practice. He has been a pioneer of New Keynesian macro models. These are models in which people are assumed to have 'rational expectations' and calculate optimal rules of behaviour, yet there is a degree of price and wage stickiness. We mean by rational expectations that people understand how the economy responds to policy behaviour, and so they make intelligent predictions of the outcomes of policies and use these predictions to decide how best to behave themselves. The sort of price and wage stickiness that Taylor studied came from overlapping contracts. His work mainly looked at wage contracts in which different groups signed contracts, typically for one year, at different times of the year (e.g. Taylor 1979). Since others had signed already and others would sign soon, each group had to think about what these other contracts would be: hence, overlapping. Following his early contributions, there have been several waves of alternative models of wage and price stickiness, but, as my Cardiff University colleague Huw Dixon has shown (Dixon and Le Bihan 2012), all of these models, when suitably generalised, give rather similar results.

The New Keynesian models that come out of these approaches have, in truth, little to do with the Keynesian models of the early post-war textbooks. They are best thought of as models based on the assumptions of microeconomics, namely, that people optimise subject to constraints and use information intelligently, but, for various practical reasons, do not change prices and wages continuously. They constitute the current generation of dynamic stochastic general equilibrium models. While it is now the fashion among non-macroeconomists to moan about their deficiencies, most macroeconomists can see little alternative to using them, while also trying to improve them as best we can. John Taylor has made considerable contributions to their development over the years.

He made a number of technical contributions to model-building in the course of this work. These contributions included work on how to solve rational expectations models and how to understand their behaviour (e.g. Fair and Taylor 1983). As part of this work, Taylor developed models of the world and the US economy along these lines and was one of a group of economists investigating the best rules that central banks could follow for monetary policy. Together with Warwick McKibbin and Dale Henderson (1993), he found that setting interest rates to react to two gaps, between inflation and its target rate (of, say, 2 per cent) and between output and its potential or normal rate, was an effective policy for not only holding inflation down but also keeping output stable. After this work in the early 1990s, Taylor examined what the Fed had done over the previous decade. He found that a rule of this kind fitted their behaviour rather well. This became known as the 'Taylor rule', and he suggested that the stability from the early 1980s could be put down to the Fed having followed this rule (Taylor 1993).

Taylor has also been active in practical policy and has done several stints in government, such as on the Council of Economic Advisers and also as a government minister for international economic policy. His advice on policy issues comes from a free-market standpoint, with accompanying emphasis on a monetary policy Taylor rule and responsible fiscal policy.

In the 2015 Hayek lecture, Taylor argues that, during the 2000s, the Fed abandoned the Taylor rule in the direction of extreme looseness. This triggered the credit and housing boom, which, in turn, created the conditions for the banking crisis. He suggests that similar policies were pursued in the UK and the euro zone, partially stimulated by excessive easing in the US. Arguably, the effect of this was spread around the world by the willingness of emerging market central banks to keep their currencies down against the dollar by buying dollars and selling their own currencies, thereby boosting their own money supplies. His main proposal for dealing with the threat of future financial crises is therefore that monetary policy should stick more closely to the Taylor rule. He is also concerned at the surge in ad hoc discretionary policy changes before and after the crisis: the huge rise in regulation, the bail-outs and special tax and spending measures. He argues that we need to respect the rule of law and have predictable economic policies if we are to enjoy economic freedom and the growth that comes with it. In general, his lecture is a plea to restore predictable rules of behaviour in policy – whether it be monetary policy, tax, public spending or regulation.

Evaluating John Taylor's particular thesis about the financial crisis

I accept Taylor's view that monetary policy in the 2000s was too loose and therefore greatly contributed to the credit and money boom, thereby worsening the bust and sowing the seeds of the financial crisis. For evidence of this, he shows how the Taylor rule would have set interest rates compared with their actual settings: the outcome is that they would definitely have been higher.

The question he does not address is whether even the Taylor rule would have generated sufficient monetary restraint in the 2000s. This is a difficult question to answer, as it requires one to produce a counterfactual projection of what would have happened to the economy had the Taylor rule been followed. This can only be done with a model of the US economy that convincingly 'fits the facts'.

As it happens, a group of us at Cardiff (Le, Meenagh and Minford 2014) have been investigating how one could model the US economy to include a role for banks and for money. To this end, we adapted the widely accepted work of others in a number of ways to achieve a good fit to the data of recent decades, including the crisis period and the 'zero bound' on interest rates. Our measure of fit is the ability of the model to replicate the behaviour of the data during these decades – a method known as indirect inference, which has considerable power in small samples.[1]

We managed to find a version of the model that passed the necessary statistical tests. We then asked it what crisis behaviour the existing policy rules, including the Taylor rule and limited money supply intervention, would generate, and whether alternative rules could reduce the incidence of crises. When it came to the Taylor rule regime, the monetary policy set-up that was modelled consisted of the Taylor rule, a mild reaction of the monetary base in support of the volume of credit in normal times and a QE reaction when the zero bound for nominal interest rates occurred. In line with what has happened in practice, the QE reaction was largely offset by the simultaneous introduction of more intrusive bank regulation, which caused banks to reduce credit. We found that, even if the Fed had followed these existing rules, crises were endemic. Following these rules also did not dampen credit and/or money booms sufficiently, nor did they lean hard enough against the subsequent recessions.

---

1   In technical language, the method involves comparing the behaviour of the data, as represented by the coefficients of general time series equations (known as a 'vector auto regression'), with the distribution of these coefficients that is implied by the model's simulated behaviour. The data-based coefficients should jointly lie inside the (say, 95 per cent) confidence bounds of this distribution for the model to pass the test.

Applying these rules in the face of repeated sequences of shocks, we found the data generated a relatively high frequency of crises – just over 20 per thousand years (a little over one every half century), roughly half of which were financial crises. A crisis is defined as a fall in output that does not return to its previous peak for at least three years. We find that crises are basically caused by real shocks, and that financial shocks alone cannot cause them. Financial shocks do, however, worsen an already-occurring crisis. So, the bottom line is that the Taylor rule is not enough to stop them.

Alternatives and complements to Taylor rules

We then examined 'beefed-up' Taylor rules: one with nominal GDP targeting and one with price level targeting. We also looked at a strong QE response to crises with the regulatory reaction in relation to bank capital eliminated. All these modifications are capable, alone or in combination, of reducing the crisis frequency dramatically. For example, nominal GDP targeting combined with the QE rule reduces the frequency of crises to a negligible 1.3 per thousand years. Table 1 shows the results.

Did the Taylor rule with inflation targeting fail during and before the crash?

Clearly, such numbers only illustrate broad directions of change. What can we make of them?

Like many macro-economists, I embraced the inflation targeting framework as being likely to give large gains in

Table 1 Simulated frequencies of crises with different monetary regimes

	Number of crises per 1,000 years	Episodes of the zero bound to nominal interest rates being reached per 1,000 years
Taylor rule	20.8	34.8
Taylor rule altered to:		
Price level target replacing inflation target	2.2	21.2
Nominal GDP target only	1.8	14.1
Price level target, plus QE in crisis, plus not tightening bank capital requirements	1.4	20.7
Nominal GDP target, plus QE in crisis, plus not tightening bank capital requirements	1.3	13.9

economic stability. Indeed, the evidence suggests that it did. However, it seems that in an inflation targeting context, the Taylor rule, even had it been rigorously followed, would have failed to avoid pretty serious instability in the 2000s. The reason seems to be that inflation did not vary enough to prompt the sort of vigorous monetary responses needed to stabilise credit booms and busts. One way of putting this is in terms of the old dictum about monetary policy made by William McChesney Martin, Chairman of the Federal Reserve, in a speech in the 1950s (Martin 1955). He suggested that the job of monetary policy was to take away the punch bowl 'just when the party was really warming up'. This was also the essence of Milton Friedman's proposal to keep the growth of the money supply stable. Unfortunately, the demand for money became hard to predict, as intermediation became more and more competitive from the 1970s onwards. This effectively caused the switch to interest-rate rules that were based on inflation and output deviations from their targets.

How can it be that these rules, which apparently worked well when they were tested out on models of the economy before they were introduced, do not work so well when it comes to creating stability in practice? In fact, Taylor rules have stabilised inflation remarkably more than they were expected to, but they have stabilised output less than they were expected to. Notably, they failed to avert the recent crisis. Taylor's answer is that central banks departed from the Taylor rule in the 2000s. Yet, according to the econometric models we have used, they may well not have done so. In fact, the application of Taylor rules may have temporarily injected more ease into the system at the wrong time. Then there were 'shocks' when policymakers deviated from the rule due to monetary judgements that were made about the economic situation. Such temporary shocks to interest rates do not invalidate the existence of the Taylor rule overall. Furthermore, when one looks at the effects of central bank action on inflation, it is very clear that the Taylor rule was operating, because inflation expectations were strongly anchored around 2 per cent in most countries: policy remained credible, and people believed that central banks would hit their targets. Indeed, our model of the US economy estimates that the Taylor rule was operating but that it was unable to control output fluctuations. So, if central banks had stuck more closely to the Taylor rule in the 2000s, it might have helped somewhat, but it may not have averted the build-up of pressures that preceded the crisis.

The reason for this seems to be that inflation deviations from target are quite small and, therefore, in conjunction with a weak Taylor rule response to the output gap, produce little monetary response to (credit) boom and the following slump. In the boom, money is not tightened enough; in the slump, the monetary ease is insufficient, notably because of hitting the zero lower bound on interest rates. The punch bowl is not produced or taken away with enough vigour. With the alternative rules of either a price level target or nominal GDP target, the necessary monetary response to get the target variable back on track is greater. As such, booms or busts in credit and monetary conditions are more easily avoided.

The previous models, which indicated strong effectiveness of the Taylor rule and inflation targeting, may not have taken account of shifts in behaviour because of the introduction of the rule itself. This point is an illustration of the Lucas (1976) critique of econometric modelling: that behaviour shifts when policy rules change. Closer to home, Charles Goodhart has emphasised this problem in monetary behaviour in 'Goodhart's Law' (Goodhart 1975). It did not occur to the proponents of the Taylor rule (including me) that the Taylor rule would not prevent credit boom and bust, because, in previous models, inflation would react sensitively to rising demand fuelled by credit growth. Unfortunately, in the world after the introduction of Taylor rules and inflation targeting, inflation moved very little

– essentially because everyone anticipated that it would be brought back to 2 per cent. The fact was that inflation expectations remained anchored to the target because the Taylor rule increased the credibility of central banks and, therefore, reinforced the belief of wage setters, financial market participants and so on that inflation would remain close to 2 per cent. This in turn meant that measured inflation stayed low, even while monetary growth was high. Even the Deutsche Bundesbank and the ECB were lulled by the new environment into ignoring their 'second pillar' of money growth.

It follows that we should be cautious about expecting too much of new rules. However, we cannot in my view avoid introducing changes to monetary rules in the light of this crisis. Furthermore, there has been much progress due to the introduction and widespread use of the Taylor rule – notably, inflation has been finally shown to be totally controllable. Thirty-five years ago, inflation was the number one problem, and governments were still clueless as to what to do about it. Now it has been conquered. But, naturally, as one problem is conquered, others come into view. We must carry on trying to deal with these problems via further changes to the rules.

John Taylor's plea for a return to predictable rules of policy

While I have argued that Taylor is too sanguine in arguing that just sticking to the Taylor rule would have been enough to prevent the crisis, in his wider remarks about the need for a return to predictability in policy, I believe that he is totally correct. This crisis has seen government behaviour at its worst, intervening all over the economy in ways quite beyond the rule of law. One thing he does not mention, but implies, is the politicisation of key economic reactions that occurred in the crisis. So eager were politicians to be involved, and to be seen by their constituents to be involved, that they intervened freely in the debate on monetary policy decisions. The Fed itself became an object of controversy and, in the fateful decision over Lehman Brothers, it seems clear that the surrounding debate about moral hazard was an important element in leading to a withdrawal of the liquidity protection that could have surrounded a quite feasible sale of Lehman. Lender of last resort facilities do create moral hazard, just as the existence of fire engines does. However, this does not mean that they are not to be used in crises, just as fire engines should be used in fires. Central banks failed to achieve an effective lender of last resort function in this crisis; this was partly due to difficulties of international coordination, but, mainly, it was due to politics and fear of politics. In fact, during 2007, and until September 2008, central banks were muddling through; but, with Lehman, things fell apart.

As Taylor remarked, we now have a mountain of (mostly useless and generally distortionary) regulation, an ongoing debate about whether government should carry on 'stimulating' the economy via fiscal activism, and a QE programme under which central banks have absorbed large amounts of government debt (about a third in the case of the UK) and driven yields on that debt down below the rate of inflation for much of the past few years. The combination of all of these policies poses a substantial threat to economic freedom. Fortunately, in the US, the UK and much of the developed world, recovery of some sort has taken hold, and normality is beginning to return, so outright socialism may be in retreat. However, in the euro zone, unemployment remains at high rates – in some countries, it is at more than 20 per cent, and recovery is weak, even non-existent. The threat of social instability leading to further socialist centralisation is non-negligible. In retrospect, the introduction of the euro can be seen, as many economists warned, to have been hugely premature.

Taylor has emphasised how crucial good policy rules are to the maintenance of economic freedom. Such rules maintain economic stability, and so contain demands to override the law. When they fail, as this crisis has shown, economic freedom and progress are threatened. Some people are hopeful that the euro zone crisis, which has turned out to be the worst product of the overall crisis, will, as a result of its severity, generate a demand for economic 'reform' (i.e. more market liberalisation). Unfortunately, the opposite is more likely. When the general economic situation is bad, losers from reform are less willing to make concessions, and gainers are less willing to compensate them. This reduces the political possibility of reform. Instead, populist remedies, such as socialist planning, can become more attractive to a desperate multitude.

Conclusions

Taylor's lecture reminded me of his many fine contributions to macroeconomics. His main contention in this lecture was focused on the crisis and how it could have been prevented. He argued that monetary policy was far too loose in the 2000s and set the world up for a financial crash fuelled by excessively high asset prices, particularly house prices. He suggested that, had the Fed followed the rule that he discovered it seems to have followed from the mid 1980s, which was later named the 'Taylor rule' after him, policy would have been sufficient to avert the crisis. While I freely concede that money was too loose and that following the Taylor rule exactly would have delivered more tightness, on the contention that the Taylor rule would have been sufficient I am doubtful. The Taylor rules followed by many central banks were unexpectedly effective in stabilising inflation, which, in turn, meant that they largely failed to stabilise credit and money growth. I have shown some model simulations which suggest that rules targeting money, credit and/or nominal GDP or the price level might have prevented the 2007–10 crisis.

Taylor also emphasised how this crisis has led to the overturning of predictable policy behaviour, to the detriment of economic freedom and long-term progress. On this, he is surely quite correct. As the euro zone part of the overall crisis has reminded us, a general collapse of stabilising policy rules leads to the threat of social instability and damages the prospects for economic liberalisation. It is fortunate that, in most of the rest of the developed world, some sort of recovery has taken hold, so that outright socialism seems to be in retreat. Nevertheless, demands for ever more government intervention on all fronts remain strong. These demands, in their most threatening form (as seen in the euro zone), are the most worrying legacy of this crisis.

References

Dixon, H. and Le Bihan, H. (2012) Generalised Taylor and generalised Calvo price and wage setting: micro-evidence with macro implications. *Economic Journal* 122(560): 532–54.

Fair, R. and Taylor, J. B. (1983) Solution and maximum likelihood estimation of dynamic rational expectations models. *Econometrica*, July, pp. 1169–85.

Goodhart, C. A. E. (1975) Problems of monetary management: the UK experience. Papers in Monetary Economics. Reserve Bank of Australia, I.

Henderson, D. W. and McKibbin, W. (1993) A comparison of some basic monetary policy regimes for open economies: implications of different degrees of instrument adjustment and wage persistence. *Carnegie-Rochester Conference Series on Public Policy* 39: 221–318.

Le, V. P. M., Meenagh, D. and Minford, P. (2014) Monetarism rides again? US monetary policy in a world of quantitative easing.Cardiff Working Paper E 2014/22. Economics Section, Cardiff Business School, Cardiff University. CEPR Discussion Paper 10250. London: CEPR.

Lucas, R. (1976) Econometric policy evaluation: a critique. In *The Phillips Curve and Labor Markets* (ed. K. Brunner and

A. Meltzer), pp. 19–46. Carnegie-Rochester Conference Series on Public Policy, Volume 1.

Martin Jr, W. M. (1955) Speech to New York Group of the Investment Bankers Association of America, 19 October, 1955.

Taylor, J. B. (1979) Staggered wage setting in a macro model. *American Economic Review* 69(2): 108–13.

Taylor, J. B. (1993) Discretion versus policy rules in practice. *Carnegie-Rochester Series on Public Policy* 39: 195–214.

4 THE NEED FOR DISCRETION AND RULES[1]

A commentary on John Taylor's lecture

Andrew G. Haldane and Amar Radia

John Taylor's contribution to public policy, especially monetary policy, has been immense. It has been the more so for Taylor's career having straddled both academia and public policy. The principles of sound policymaking that Taylor has helped develop have infused central bank thinking the world over. It is difficult to think of any other economist whose name is attached to three central concepts in macroeconomics: the Taylor principle, the Taylor curve and the Taylor rule.[2]

---

1   The authors thank Richard Blows, Shiv Chowla, George Murphy and Michael McMahon for their comments and contributions.

2   The Taylor principle states that nominal interest rates respond more than one-for-one to a change in inflation. It was implicit in Taylor (1993) but first defined by Woodford (1999). The Taylor curve maps out the relationship between fluctuations in inflation and fluctuations in output – 'a "second order" Phillips curve which is not vertical in the long-run' (Taylor 1979). The Taylor rule (Taylor 1993) is a simple equation that describes a relationship between nominal interest rates and several key macroeconomic variables.

In light of our experience over the past 40 years or so, since Taylor first began work on monetary policy regimes, now is a good time for a stocktake. What have we learned from this experience? Specifically, what have we learned about two principles that have underpinned Taylor's work: the virtues of rules-based policy decision-making in general, and the usefulness of simple monetary policy rules in particular?

Rules and discretion revisited

The road to constrained discretion

The debate about rules versus discretion is several centuries old.[3] In the monetary policy sphere, the issue dates back to Simons (1936). It has now been at the very centre of public policy debate for over half a century.[4] In the early 1960s, Milton Friedman proposed a simple 'k%' rule for the money supply (Friedman 1960). This was intended in part as a safeguard against the fine-tuning of the economy, which might amplify, rather than smooth, the cycle. More fundamentally, it was about avoiding major policy errors, the likes of which Friedman believed had worsened the Great Depression.

---

3   It may even be much older. In Plato's *Statesman*, the Eleatic Stranger initially believes it prudent to entrust power to individuals possessed with genuine wisdom. But, upon realising that few possess such wisdom, he begins to think that rules, however inflexible, may be a more sensible alternative.

4   Simons (1936) referred to 'rules versus authorities'.

The great inflation of the 1970s, and the implied failure of discretionary monetary regimes after the breakdown of Bretton Woods, appeared to add empirical weight to Friedman's arguments. Further theoretical weight came from Kydland and Prescott's 1977 paper, which showed that discretionary policymakers are not just error-prone but may be inclined to generate systematically above-target inflation – an 'inflation bias'. Any discretionary promise risked proving time inconsistent. A central bank attempting to promise low inflation would always find itself tempted to generate a surprise bout of inflation today in order to boost output above potential. Recognising that, the public would not believe the central bank's promise, instead expecting permanently above-target inflation. The outcome would be just that. Avoiding inflationary temptation – or achieving time consistency – called for pre-committed, or rule-like, forms of monetary anchor.

At the same time, a separate strand of research was pointing in another direction. Pre-commitment came with costs. If it resulted in important information on the economy being ignored, policy could become too inflexible. That was the real lesson, it was argued, from the breakdown of Bretton Woods and, before it, the Gold Standard. At least in simple risk-based settings, the optimal monetary policy was fully state-contingent. That is, it depended on the prevailing economic conditions. And, because the state of the economy varies so much over time, and in an unpredictable way, simple rules are inadequate. The state-contingent approach meant using all available information, alongside policymakers' judgements, to adjust policy over time and across states of nature (as is outlined, for example, in King (1994)).

This fully state-contingent approach to optimal policy was itself not without problems. One of those was that it, too, may be time inconsistent (Kydland and Prescott 1977; Barro and Gordon 1983). Another came in defining the optimal information set, especially when this also comprised something as opaque as policymakers' judgements. A third, closely related problem was the lack of transparency, and, hence, predictability, that such a complex rule was likely to entail.

The two sides of this coin became known as the 'credibility–flexibility trade-off' in the design of policy frameworks (Lohmann 1992). A state-invariant rule (such as Friedman's) sat at one end of this trade-off, while a fully state-contingent approach sat at the other. In between sat a range of potential approaches, blending rules and discretion. In a number of theoretical settings, these interior solutions were found to be preferred to either of the extremes.

In practice, policy frameworks have tended to settle in the intermediate zone over the past few decades. That is why they have often become known as regimes of 'constrained discretion' (Bernanke 2003). Under such regimes, policy is set judgmentally rather than mechanically, but it is also set within constraints specified ex ante and enforced ex post. These constraints surround the specification of policy objectives, the mechanics of policy decision-making and the transparency and accountability of policy actions. In that way, constrained discretion is intended to confer flexibility, while preserving commitment.

Today, the regimes for monetary, macro-prudential and micro-prudential policy in many countries can reasonably be characterised as constrained discretion regimes, though the balance often differs across the three arms of policy. For example, in the UK, monetary policy has a clear, quantitative policy objective (an inflation target), a clear decision-maker (the Bank of England's Monetary Policy Committee, or MPC) and clear and transparent procedures for making and reporting their decisions. The features are defined in statute and constitute the constraints within which the MPC's policy judgement is exercised. These features are shared by many monetary policy regimes around the world.

Institutional solutions to discretionary biases

In the UK, some of these institutional features are also present in the regimes that have been introduced for macro-prudential and micro-prudential policy. Both have clear, if non-quantitative, objectives defined ex ante in statute. Both have clear, delegated decision-makers (the Bank's Financial Policy Committee and the Board of the Prudential Regulation Authority, respectively). Both have transparency and accountability of decision-making from these bodies. Although there is not the same degree of consensus as in the monetary policy sphere, these features have also been replicated internationally in a number of countries since the crisis.

What this means, practically, is that although the rules-versus-discretion debate remains active today, it is far less polarised than at many times in the past. The debate today is less one of principle. Rather, it is centred on specific institutional features and safeguards. What is the right specification of the policy objective? What information and models are being used to make decisions? How much transparency is optimal?

These institutional features serve, in part, as a safeguard against the pitfalls of discretionary policy regimes. Take, for example, inflation biases. These were one of the original motivations for rule-like monetary policy. Yet many now see the time-inconsistency problem as overblown (Blinder 1998; King 2000). One reason for this is the success in meeting inflation targets over the past 20 years or so. Another is the international trend towards delegating monetary policymaking to operationally independent central banks. Independent central banks have fewer incentives to inflate than governments if they are controlling monetary policy directly (Bean 1998).[5]

These policy lessons have since found their way into the design of other policy frameworks – for example, macro-prudential and micro-prudential policy. In many countries today, including the UK, these policies have been delegated to an independent, arms-length institution, often the central bank (International Monetary Fund 2013). This is recognition that the time-consistency problem is every bit as acute when taming crises as it is when taming inflation (Haldane 2013).

---

5 A range of studies (Alesina and Summers 1993; Cuikerman 1992) find that measures of central bank independence appear to be associated with lower inflation outcomes).

As for the benefits of flexibility, it has recently been argued that the array of data and analysis used by central banks simply cannot be easily summarised into a single, simple rule – central banks possess 'non-ruleable' information (Kocherlakota 2014). For example, Kocherlakota argues that when the variance of privately held information on inflationary pressures is large relative to the inflation bias that central banks might have, discretion may be the superior approach to policy.[6]

Just how non-ruleable is central banks' information? In other words, to what extent could central banks' decision-making processes be summarised by rules? One guide is perhaps provided by looking at the information content of central bankers' deliberations. Recently, Michael McMahon and Stephen Hansen have conducted detailed text-based analyses of monetary policy decisions based on the published minutes of policy meetings. For example, Figure 12 plots the relative importance of four topics discussed by the Bank of England's MPC relating to the determinants of inflation (commodity prices, the exchange rate, wages and inflation expectations) between 2004 and 2014.

As might be expected, the relative importance of each topic waxes and wanes. The amount of attention devoted to commodity prices was high in 2005 and 2012. But, at other times, the exchange rate or inflation expectations were the dominant topic of conversation for policymakers. Overall, this suggests that the MPC has exhibited a significant degree of flexibility in how they have weighted these

---

6   Building on work by Athey et al. (2005).

Figure 12 Incidence of topics affecting inflation discussed by the MPC

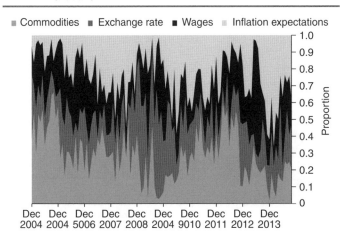

■ Commodities ■ Exchange rate ■ Wages ▨ Inflation expectations

Source: Bank calculations. This chart shows the estimated split of the MPC's discussion of topics relating to the determinants of inflation to those topics, according to the MPC minutes. The estimation of the topics, and the allocation of each set of minutes across topics, is completed using latent Dirichlet allocation.

developments, flexibility which may have been difficult to codify in a fixed rule.

An alternative interpretation of this evidence is that its highlights a lack of policy consistency and predictability. Calomiris et al. (2015) argue that the US Federal Reserve's focus on the labour market since the crisis has been misguided, with undue prominence given to unemployment and wage growth, neither of which is an especially good predictor of inflation. Figure 13 shows the proportion of MPC discussions accounted for by a combination of wages and unemployment. Since late 2010, the focus on the

Figure 13 Incidence of topics linked to the labour market discussed by the MPC

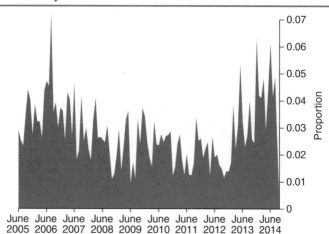

Source: Bank calculations. This chart shows the estimated proportion of the MPC's discussion of topics relating to the labour market, according to the MPC minutes. The estimation of the topics, and the allocation of each set of minutes across topics, is completed using latent Dirichlet allocation.

labour market has increased, though as a fraction of the committee's time it remains fairly modest.

Even if inflation biases are not as great today as was once thought likely, other behavioural biases in decision-making may be important. As the literature on behavioural economics makes clear, these biases are legion (Haldane 2014). One decision-making defect highlighted by Taylor is activism bias – the desire to intervene excessively. This concept is closely related to overconfidence bias, since the urge to fine-tune is likely to be greatest when confidence in your abilities is inflated.

Figure 14 Distribution of inflation and growth outcomes relative to forecast

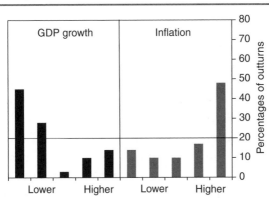

Source: Bank calculations. For further details on the methodology, please see Hackworth et al. (2013). This chart shows the dispersion of inflation and GDP growth outturns since 2007 Q3 across the quintiles of the one-year-ahead Inflation Report fan chart distributions up to the February 2014 Inflation Report.

There is evidence of overconfidence bias in many decision-making settings (Shiller 2000). Pre-crisis, there is certainly some evidence of central banks having systematically underestimated risks to the economy during the 'Great Moderation'. The Bank of England doubled the width of its forecast fan charts for output growth and inflation after the crisis. Despite this widening, outturns for both have continued to fall in the tails of their distributions (Figure 14).

Some of these errors are inevitable, given the uncertainties of forecasting; but there is a need to be mindful, too, of other explanations. These include groupthink – a tendency to conform in our ways of thinking within groups (Janis 1982) – and confirmation bias – a tendency to discard information that does not conform with prior views (Wason 1960). How do we guard against these biases in policy decision-making?

In other decision-making settings, there are some well-known institutional safeguards against these psychological biases. For example, decision-making by committee reduces the risk of confirmation bias. And having a committee composed of members whose experience is diverse, who are individually accountable and who are exposed to challenges from outside can mitigate groupthink (Sibert 2006).

These institutional safeguards have tended to find their way into policy decision-making at central banks over the past few decades. For example, at the Bank of England, the three arms of policy – monetary, macro-prudential and micro-prudential – are executed by separate committees. Committee members are drawn from both inside and outside the bank, with diverse sets of experience, and each member is individually accountable to Parliament. This committee structure should reduce the risk of groupthink and confirmation bias.

Evidence on monetary policy decision-making behaviour in practice is broadly consistent with that hypothesis. The majority of MPC meetings have seen at least one member dissent from a decision (Haldane 2014). The chairman of the MPC has been outvoted on an interest rate decision on a number of occasions. And, over the past few years, further efforts have been made to strengthen the transparency of the MPC's forecast and decision-making process (McKeown and Paterson 2014; Warsh 2014).

To sum up, policymakers internationally have heeded, and have been right to heed, the core lesson of Taylor's work: policy should be set systematically. This has been achieved by ongoing institutional evolution in regimes of constrained policy discretion, balancing the needs of credibility and flexibility. At the same time, if recent history is any guide, these policy frameworks will need to continue to evolve in response to events and experience – good and bad – if they are to achieve an appropriate balance between credibility and flexibility. That is particularly true of micro- and macro-prudential regimes, which, in institutional terms, remain in their infancy.

Monetary policy rules in practice

Taylor's famous 1993 paper, which introduced the Taylor rule, contained an important proviso: 'simple, algebraic formulations of such rules cannot and should not be mechanically followed by policymakers' (Taylor 1993). Two decades on, how are monetary policy rules being used in practice, and what have we learnt?

Three big virtues

Even simple rules have been found to be very useful in the policy formulation process. Taylor rules are routinely examined by policymakers in central banks the world over. They feature prominently in central bankers' speeches and frequently form the backbone of external commentary on monetary policy. There are three big virtues possessed by Taylor rules that might help explain their popularity.

Firstly, Taylor rules capture the essence of modern macroeconomics. Monetary policy responds to deviations of inflation from target and output from its potential. These two objectives appear in the standard policymaker loss function in the academic literature. They also appear in the statutory mandates assigned to most central banks. Under certain conditions, those objectives can be shown to be consistent with maximising the expected utility of households (Woodford 1999).

Taylor rules also embody the notion that, at times, policymakers may face a trade-off between these objectives. This trade-off can be represented by the Taylor curve – the set of output and inflation variability pairs possible under different monetary policy reaction functions (Taylor 1979). Situations in which policy can simultaneously keep inflation at target and output at potential – the so-called divine coincidence – are relatively rare. By imposing relative weights on inflation and the output gap, the Taylor rule offers a simple way of making choices from this menu.

Taylor rules are also a means of assessing whether monetary policy is adhering to the Taylor principle – that nominal rates should increase at least one-for-one with inflation. Or, put differently, any monetary policy reaction function that violates the Taylor principle is likely to set in motion an inflationary spiral. Empirical evidence suggests that such violations were common during the late 1960s and 1970s, when inflation was high and rising (see, for example, Clarida et al. 2000).

Secondly, in part due to their simplicity and transparency, Taylor rules are more likely to deliver robustness in decision-making – for example, in the face of model uncertainty. A range of studies (Taylor 1999; Levin and Williams 2003) has demonstrated that a simple Taylor rule is likely, on average, to deliver better performance across a range of models than either a complex rule or a fully optimal policy. In other words, a Taylor rule can serve as a safeguard against model misspecification and uncertainty.

The intuition behind this result is as follows. The optimal rule in any single model will exploit features of that model to generate better outcomes, so it is likely to be complex. But, in different model settings, these over-fitted complex rules may perform poorly. As the gains in moving from simple rules to optimal rules within any model are typically fairly modest, simple rules tend to be preferable *across* models. This carries the implication that Taylor rules may be especially useful as policy guideposts at times of structural change.

Thirdly, Taylor rules have become essential modelling devices for policymakers. In most central bank models, the baseline path for monetary policy is generated by a Taylor-like rule. This closes the model, ensuring the price level is determinate. Moreover, because the Taylor rule provides a reasonable fit of how policymakers have tended to behave over the past, it also captures the essence of how policy might be set in practice.

Judgement remains central

While the past two decades have taught us a great deal about the usefulness of Taylor rules, they have also highlighted some of their limitations. To explore those, consider the general form of the Taylor rule:

$$i_t = r_t^* + \pi_t + \theta_\pi(\pi_t - \pi^*) + \theta_y(y_t - \bar{y}_t).$$

In Taylor's original work, he set r^* (the equilibrium rate of interest) to 2 per cent and θ_π (the weight on the difference between inflation and the target) and θ_y (the weight on the output gap) to 0.5. With an inflation target of 2 per cent, the canonical Taylor rule is thus

$$i_t = 2 + \pi_t + 0.5(\pi_t - 2) + 0.5(y_t - \bar{y}_t).$$

In simple terms, this means that the interest rate should be set at 2 per cent, plus the rate of inflation, plus half the difference between actual inflation and the target rate of inflation (2 per cent), plus half the difference between actual output and trend output. If inflation was at target and output at potential, the prevailing real rate of interest would therefore be 2 per cent.

If we calculate potential output as an extrapolation of trend growth rates (as in Taylor's original paper), this gives the Taylor rule path for UK interest rates shown in Figure 15. At least up until the crisis, it shows a reasonable fit relative to actual policy rates: the Taylor rule path rarely deviates from actual rates by more than one percentage point. But, after the crisis, we see a sharp and significant deviation, with the Taylor rule implying a much lower level of interest rates. By 2015, this gap is over eight percentage points.

This highlights why adherence to a particular calibration of the Taylor rule has the potential to lead policymakers

Figure 15 Actual and Taylor rule paths for UK interest rates

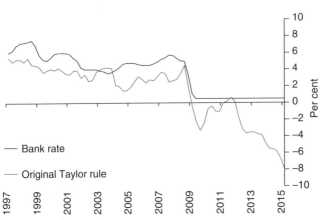

Bank rate

Original Taylor rule

Sources: Bank of England, Office for National Statistics (ONS) and Bank calculations.

astray. With the output gap calculated as the deviation of GDP from its long-run average, the implied output gap in the UK today would be around 18 per cent of GDP. In practice, the MPC judge it to be less than 1 per cent.

Potential output growth is susceptible to a range of real shocks that monetary policy cannot neatly offset. These have the potential to cause permanent shifts in trend supply (Woodford 2001). Financial crises in the past and present have been a prime example of such shocks. Adjustment for these shifts is important when assessing potential output, which inevitably requires a degree of judgement and a range of models.

Figure 16 shows a Taylor rule based on a different, judgement-based, measure of the output gap. Since the crisis, it has deviated from the historical trend-based path by between four and eight percentage points. Differences on that scale could have major consequences for policy. One reading of the 1970s is that, rather than disobeying the Taylor principle, policymakers in fact misjudged the size of the output gap (Orphanides 2003).

Once a policymaker has an estimate of the output gap, there is then a question about the relative weights to place on output and inflation gaps in a Taylor rule. Taylor's original formulation set both to 0.5. Indeed, one of his arguments in favour of a lower weight on the output gap is that the rule then became more robust to output gap mismeasurement (Taylor and Williams 2009).

Figure 16 Taylor rule paths for UK interest rates with different judgements about the output gap

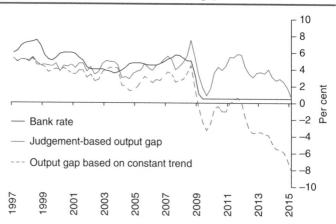

Sources: Bank of England, ONS, projections consistent with MPC judgements in the August Inflation Reports and Bank calculations.

Janet Yellen has argued that a coefficient of 1 on the output gap and 0.5 on the inflation gap – a 'balanced-approach rule' – is more consistent with the Federal Open Market Committee's mandate (Yellen 2012). Figure 17 shows the level of interest rates that would have prevailed under these two rules. While, in general, they track each other fairly closely, at times during the crisis they have suggested interest rate differences of as much as two percentage points. So, while the Taylor rule offers one way of navigating the output–inflation trade-off, policymakers' preferences in practice may be apt to differ in terms of how to construct the rule. Such differences may have significant effects on the level of interest

Figure 17 Taylor rules for UK interest rates with different judgements about weight on output gap

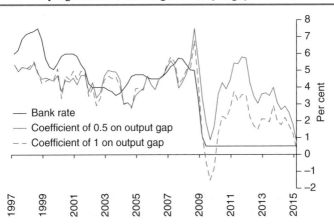

Sources: Bank of England, ONS, projections consistent with MPC judgements in the August Inflation Reports and Bank calculations.

rates, which will be different depending on where we are in the cycle.

A further issue, of particular relevance in the current environment, is how to calibrate the equilibrium interest rate, or intercept term, in the Taylor rule. While the original rule contained a time-invariant rate of 2 per cent above inflation, as Woodford (2001) notes: 'in reality there may be substantial variation in the natural rate. Failure to adjust the intercept to track variation in the natural rate of interest will result in fluctuations in inflation and the output gap'.

In the aftermath of the crisis, with big shortfalls in output across advanced economies, the focus for policy-makers was initially on the size of the output gap. More recently, however, central banks' attention has turned to the appropriate setting of the equilibrium rate – sometimes known colloquially as r^*. If this has changed, then applying a Taylor rule featuring an equilibrium rate of 2 per cent will lead policymakers astray.

Taylor's view is that 2 per cent remains 'about right' for r^* (Taylor 2014). But financial markets appear to take a somewhat different view. Global medium- and long-term real interest rates have been trending downwards for over 30 years (King and Low 2014). This poses a challenge to the assumption that the equilibrium rate is static over time. Moreover, even medium-term global real rates have entered negative territory in a number of countries. This, too, poses a challenge to an assumed 2 per cent equilibrium rate.

Figure 18 shows the Taylor rule under two different formulations of the equilibrium rate: one based on measures of real interest rates extracted from financial markets, and another that adjusts equilibrium interest rates for movements in the risky credit spread charged to borrowers. Clearly, this has material implications for the setting of policy, with the span of possible policy rates suggested by the different methods of setting the equilibrium rate currently around 2.5 percentage points.

A final area of judgement surrounds whether Taylor rules should be forward looking. In most versions of the Taylor rule, policy responds to current levels of inflation

Figure 18 Taylor rules paths for interest rates with different judgements about _r_*

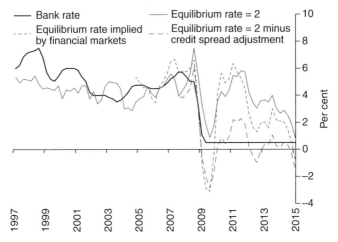

Sources: Bank of England, Bloomberg, ONS, projections consistent with MPC judgements in the August Inflation Reports and Bank calculations. Data for market real interest rates is derived from nominal bond yields deflated using inflation swaps. An adjustment is made to account for the difference between the Retail Price Index (RPI) and the Consumer Price Index (CPI). For more details on the calculation of the measure of credit spreads, please see Butt and Pugh (2014).

and the output gap. But monetary policy is typically felt to be forward looking. The predominant monetary policy strategy at major central banks is sometimes described as 'inflation forecast targeting' (Svensson 1997). In other words, the policy interest rate is set to ensure that the forecast for inflation is in line with the target, rather than responding to its current level. Central bank practice is consistent with this: in a third of the MPC's forecasts over the past decade, the central tendency has been for inflation to lie – to one decimal place – at the 2 per cent inflation target two years ahead (Figure 19).

Empirical simulations of different sorts of policy rule – 'feedback' rules, such as the Taylor rule, and 'feed-forward' rules, such as inflation-forecast-targeting – have tended to suggest that the latter formulations may be preferable in stabilising inflation and output (Battini and Haldane 1999). Moreover, as Figure 20 shows, these different formulations can lead to quite different settings for interest rates. During the crisis, they deviated by as much as three to four percentage points.

These deviations were also an important point of policy debate during the pre-crisis period. Taylor (2007) argues that monetary policy in the US was too loose between 2002 and 2006, as implied by his original Taylor rule. But Bernanke (2010) counters that, according to a forward-looking version of the Taylor rule that involved setting the interest rate based on the deviation of the inflation forecast from the target, policy was set appropriately. For the UK, as Figure 20 shows, policy if anything looks to have been a little tight rather than loose before the crisis,

Figure 19 Bank of England inflation forecasts

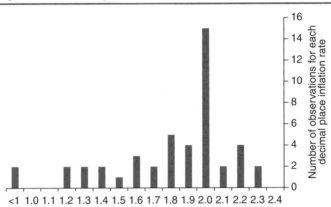

Source: Bank of England. The chart shows the distribution of two-year-ahead inflation forecasts, conditioned on market expectations of interest rates, to each decimal place.

regardless of whether the rule is forward looking or backward looking.

The key theme is that using Taylor rules as a guide to policy requires judgement. The debate over policy before the crisis focused on whether the Taylor rule should be forward looking (Bernanke 2010). In the aftermath, attention turned to the size of, and the appropriate weight on, the output gap (Yellen 2012). Today, the hot topic is the level of r^* (Haldane 2014). All of these require judgements that are often difficult.

Depending on which series of judgements a policymaker makes, the policy prescribed by a Taylor rule can differ greatly. To illustrate that, Figure 21 shows the set of

Taylor rules that can be generated by different combinations of the inputs considered in Figure 16, Figure 17, Figure 18 and Figure 20. This range was wide before the crisis and even wider today.

So, where does this leave us? Taylor rules can play a very useful role as a benchmark for monetary policy. In practice, in many countries, this is exactly how they have been used. Taylor rules can helpfully focus attention on the core features of the economy – the output gap, the output/inflation trade-off, equilibrium rates and the forecast horizon for policymakers – where judgements by monetary policymakers are most acute.

Figure 20 Taylor rules paths for interest rates with different judgements about forward lookingness

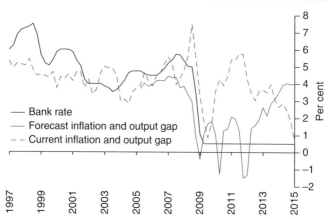

Sources: Bank of England, ONS, projections consistent with MPC judgements in the August Inflation Reports and Bank calculations.

The key word here is judgement. Too mechanical an approach to calibrating these concepts runs the risk of policymakers going astray. While this discretion is not costless, slavishly following a mechanical rule would probably be worse, and, during the course of the recent crisis, it would almost certainly have been worse.

Figure 21 Range of possible Taylor rules based on different judgements

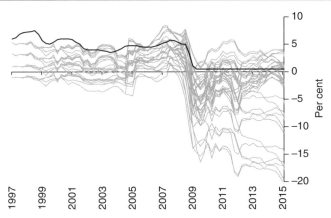

Sources: Bank of England, Bloomberg, ONS, projections consistent with MPC judgements in the August Inflation Reports and Bank calculations. The chart shows 36 Taylor rules, each of which is constructed using a different combination of assumptions about the coefficient on the output gap (0.5 or 1); the size of the output gap (calculated using pre-crisis trend or judgement); r^* (2, 2 minus a credit spread adjustment, or the level implied by financial markets); and forward lookingness (current inflation and the output gap or a two-year-ahead forecast of inflation and one-year-ahead forecast of the output gap).

Concluding remarks

It is hard to exaggerate how much of a leap forward the Taylor rule, and Taylor's work on rule-based decision-making, has been for economic modelling in general and monetary policy in particular. Taylor rules, and their descendants, are playing a key policy role. This role is enhanced, not diminished, by them being used alongside policymakers' judgements.

The Taylor rule also sets a useful standard when designing new, more fledgling, policy frameworks. One such framework is macro-prudential policy. Taylor is sceptical about this new policy apparatus, in part because he believes it may be unnecessary if monetary policy were to be appropriately set, and in part because macro-prudential policy, as currently executed, could be seen as too discretionary.

We have greater sympathy on the second of these points than the first. Pre-crisis experience provides a compelling case study of how monetary policy, however well executed, may be insufficient to forestall imbalances in the financial sector. Not only would monetary policy have been potentially ineffective in correcting these imbalances, the act of doing so – by raising interest rates – would have come at the expense of a damaging loss of output and employment (Haldane 2014).

Counterfactual simulations of the economy and the financial system with monetary and macro-prudential policies acting in harness tend to confirm this conjecture. Having monetary policy target financial stability, as well as price stability, generates an undesirable trade-off between these objectives. If monetary policy is overburdened with financial stability objectives, macro-stability suffers. But adding macro-prudential policy to the mix loosens this constraint, enabling both objectives to be met (Haldane 2015).

These counter-factual simulations posit a macro-prudential policy rule – for example, adjusting banks' capital in line with credit-to-GDP ratios, credit spreads, or estimates of likely losses in a stress. Macro-prudential policy in practice does not have a clear benchmark – such as the Taylor rule – against which it can be easily assessed. As monetary policy experience demonstrates, that can generate time inconsistency and unpredictability. Over time, as with monetary policy, there is scope for developing benchmark macro-prudential rules that could reduce these risks.

References

Alesina, A. and Summers, L. (1993) Central bank independence and macroeconomic performance: some comparative evidence. *Journal of Money, Credit and Banking* 25(2): 151–62.

Athey, S., Atkeson, A. and Kehoe, P. (2005) The optimal degree of discretion in monetary policy. *Econometrica* 73(5): 1431–75.

Barrow, R. and Gordon, D. (1983) Rules, discretion and reputation in model of monetary policy. Working Paper 1079. National Bureau of Economic Research.

Batini, N. and Haldane, A. (1999) Forward-looking rules for monetary policy. In *Monetary Policy Rules* (ed. J. Taylor), pp. 157–202. University of Chicago Press.

Bernanke, B. (2003) '"Constrained discretion" and monetary policy'. Speech at Money Marketeers. New York, NY.

Blinder, A. (1998) *Central Banking in Theory and Practice*. Cambridge, MA: MIT Press.

Butt, N. and Pugh, A. (2014) Credit spreads: capturing credit conditions facing households and firms. *Bank of England Quarterly Bulletin* 54(2): 137–47.

Calomiris, C., Ireland, P. and Levy, M. (2015) Guidelines for policymaking and communications during normalization. Shadow Open Market Committee.

Clarida, R., Gali, J. and Gertler, M. (1998) Monetary policy and macroeconomic stability: evidence and some theory. *The Quarterly Journal of Economics* 115(1): 147–180.

Cukierman, A. (1992) *Central Bank Strategy, Credibility, and Independence: Theory and Evidence*. Cambridge, MA: MIT Press.

Friedman, M. (1960) *A Program for Monetary Stability*. New York, NY: Fordham University Press.

Haldane, A. (2013) Why institutions matter (more than ever). Speech at Centre for Research on Socio-Cultural Change Annual Conference. London.

Haldane, A. (2014) Twin Peaks. Speech at Kenilworth Chamber of Trade Business Breakfast. Warwickshire.

Haldane, A. (2015) On microscopes and telescopes. Speech at Lorentz Centre Workshop on Socio-Economic Complexity.Leiden.

International Monetary Fund (2013) Key aspects of macroprudential policy. http://www.imf.org/external/np/pp/eng/2013/061013b.pdf

Janis, I. (1982) *Groupthink: Psychological Studies of Policy Decisions and Fiascoes*, 2nd edn. New York: Houghton Mifflin.

King, M. (1994) Monetary policy in the UK. *Fiscal Studies* 15(3): 109–28

King, M. (2000) Monetary policy: theory in practice. Address by Mervyn King.

King, M. and Low, D. (2014). Measuring the 'world' real interest rate. Working Paper 19887. National Bureau of Economic Research.

Kocherlakota, N. (2014) Rules versus discretion: a reconsideration. Speech at Korea–America Economic Association. Boston, MA.

Kydland, F. and Prescott, E. (1977) Rules rather than discretion: the inconsistency of optimal plans. *Journal of Political Economy* 85(3): 473–92.

Levin, A. and Williams, J. (2003) Robust monetary policy with competing reference models. *Journal of Monetary Economics* 50(5): 945–75.

Lohmann, S. (1992) Optimal commitment in monetary policy: credibility versus flexibility. *American Economic Review* 82: 273–86.

McKeown, J. and Paterson, L. (2014) Enhancing the transparency of the Bank of England's Inflation Report. http://www.voxeu.org/article/enhancing-transparency-bank-england-s-inflation-report

Orphanides, A. (2003) Historical monetary policy analysis and the Taylor rule. *Journal of Monetary Economics* 50: 983–1022.

Shiller, R. (2000) *Irrational Exuberance*. Princeton, NJ: Princeton University Press.

Sibert, A. (2006) Central banking by committee. *International Finance* 9(2): 145–68.

Simons, H. (1936) 'Rules versus Authorities in Monetary Policy' Journal of Political Economy 44(1): 1-30

Svensson, L. (1997) Inflation forecast targeting: implementing and monitoring inflation targets. *European Economic Review* 41(6): 1111–46.

Taylor, J. (1979) Estimation and control of a macroeconomic model with rational expectations. *Econometrica* 47(5): 1267–86.

Taylor, J. (1993) Discretion versus policy rules in practice. *Carnegie-Rochester Conference Series on Public Policy* 39: 195–214.

Taylor, J. (1999) An historical analysis of monetary policy rules. Working Paper 6768. National Bureau of Economic Research.

Taylor, J. (2007) Housing and monetary policy. Working Paper 13682. National Bureau of Economic Research.

Taylor, J. (2014) Terminal policy rates: hot, cold, and about right. Blog Post, *Economics One*. http://economicsone.com/2014/08/29/terminal-policy-rates-hot-cold-and-about-right/.

Taylor, J. and Williams, J. (2010) Simple and robust rules for monetary policy. In *Handbook of Monetary Economics* (ed. B. Friedman and M. Wooford), pp. 829–59. Amsterdam: Elsevier.

Warsh, K. (2014) *Transparency and the Bank of England's Monetary Policy Committee*. London: Bank of England.

Wason, P. (1960) On the failure to eliminate hypotheses in a conceptual task. *Quarterly Journal of Experimental Psychology* 12: 129–40.

Woodford, M. (1999) Optimal monetary policy inertia. Working Paper 7261. National Bureau of Economic Research.

Woodford, M. (2001) The Taylor rule and optimal monetary policy. *American Economic Review* 91(2): 232–7.

Yellen, J. (2012) Perspectives on monetary policy. Speech at Boston Economic Club Dinner. Boston, MA.

5 A REJOINDER

John B. Taylor

I am deeply grateful to Patrick Minford, and to Andy Haldane and Amar Radia, for thoughtfully commenting on my Hayek lecture, and I thank Philip Booth for the opportunity to respond briefly.

Patrick Minford begins his remarks with a useful summary of the overall framework that I have used to analyse macroeconomic policy over the years and in the lecture. He is largely in agreement with the approach and with the conclusion of my talk that there are significant benefits to be had from predictable rules-based monetary policies, and that deviating from them has been harmful.

He also agrees with the bigger point of my talk: that policy deviations from the basic principle of economic freedom are also harmful. This goes well beyond monetary policy and includes all types of economic policy: fiscal policy, regulatory policy, tax policy, international economic policy and so on. As he so clearly puts it, 'a mountain of (mostly useless and generally distortionary) regulation' combined with fiscal activism and unprecedented monetary interventions 'poses a substantial threat to economic freedom.'

He questions, however, whether adhering to the particular monetary policy rule mentioned in the paper would have prevented the financial crisis and the large downturn in 2008 and 2009. While freely conceding that, in the years before the crisis, 'money was too loose and that following the Taylor rule exactly would have delivered more tightness', he is doubtful 'about the contention that the Taylor rule would have been sufficient' to prevent the crisis. In other words, he believes the Taylor rule pointed in the right direction, but not forcefully enough.

Patrick Minford goes well beyond a mere statement of opinion, however. He conducts and reports on an interesting quantitative study with his colleagues Le and Meenagh at Cardiff University of alternative policy rules, using a new and recently updated empirical macroeconomic model. He finds that there are alternative policy rules that can reduce the chances of big fluctuations in the economy. These are 'beefed-up' Taylor rules that tend to react more forcefully and, thereby, would have been more reactive in the run-up to the crisis.

In my view, Patrick Minford's quantitative research is exactly what policymakers need to determine the best road forward for monetary policy in the future. Indeed, it was the kind of research that suggested that policymakers ought not to deviate from policy rules in the first place. And it is clearly appropriate to try to improve on models and policy rules as Patrick Minford has done.

Of course, the research raises other questions. Uncertainty in measuring real variables would suggest smaller rather than larger policy responses. There is also the need to check for robustness using other models. I have argued that regulatory lapses were an additional factor in the global financial crisis, so it was not only monetary policy anyway. But there is no reason not to modify or adjust any policy rule, including the Taylor rule, if that is what research and experience suggests is appropriate.

Andrew Haldane and Amar Radia also begin with a review of the general macroeconomic framework I use that leads to policy rules, and they are generally approving of the approach, emphasising how the research on policy rules has been a great benefit to policymakers in many countries. They also clearly explain the Taylor rule and they put it in a historical context, going back as far as Plato.

Much of their commentary delves into the basic rules-versus-discretion debate in monetary policy, and they tend to focus on problems with rules in practice. They argue in favour of an alternative approach called constrained discretion, a term used to distinguish the approach from a rules-based policy for the instruments, such as the interest rate or the money supply. The idea is that all one really needs for effective policymaking is a goal such as an inflation target and/or an unemployment target, if there is a dual mandate as in the US. With a goal in mind, you do whatever it takes with the policy instruments to achieve that goal. You do not need to develop or specify a strategy or a policy rule for the policy instruments. If you want to hold the interest rate well below the level a policy rule would suggest, then it is okay as long as you can justify it at the time in terms of the goal.

'Constrained discretion' is an appealing term, and it may reduce discretion in some ways. However, it has not, in my view, led to a move towards rules, as the term might suggest. Having a specific numerical goal or objective function is not a rule for the instruments of policy. Relying solely on constrained discretion has, in fact, resulted in a huge amount of discretion, and that has not worked well for monetary policy. David Papell of the University of Houston has shown empirically that US economic performance has been good during periods of rules-based policy and not so good in more discretionary periods (Nikolsko-Rzhevskyy et al. 2014).

A second part of Haldane and Radia's comment focuses on how the Taylor rule recommendations for the interest rate depend crucially on estimates of the output gap and the equilibrium interest rate. I have argued that the output gap should be based on a good estimate of potential output, and that 2 per cent is a good estimate of the equilibrium rate of interest.

Haldane and Radia are correct that these estimates are very uncertain, but, in my view, the uncertainty problem does not favour discretion over rules in practice. A policymaker relying on pure discretion needs to have a sense of where the real GDP and the interest rate are relative to their equilibrium levels. Moreover, a policy rule framework is a good way to discuss and assess this uncertainty.

The time-inconsistency argument in favour of rules is downplayed in the commentary, but it is only one of a host of reasons why monetary policy based more on rules and less on discretion is desirable. A policy rule can make explaining monetary policy decisions to the public or to students of public policy much easier. A policy rule is less subject to political pressure than discretion: if monetary policy appears to be run in an ad hoc rather than a systematic way, then politicians may argue that they can be just as ad hoc and interfere with monetary policy decisions. A monetary policy rule that shows how the instruments of policy are set is less subject to political pressure.

In addition, policy rules reduce uncertainty by describing future policy actions more clearly. Rules are a good way to instruct new central bankers in the art and science of monetary policy; in fact, it is for exactly this reason that new central bankers frequently find such policy rules useful for assessing their decisions. Policy rules for instrument settings also allow for more accountability. Because monetary policy works with a long and variable lag, it is difficult simply to look at inflation and determine if policymakers are doing a good job. Policy rules for the instrument also provide a useful baseline for historical comparisons.

In sum, while Haldane and Radia helpfully point out a number of important problems that must be tackled when implementing monetary policy rules, the problems are not enough to overcome the many advantages of policy rules, nor, in the bigger picture, the more general advantages of predictable policies based on the rule of law and the other key principles of economic freedom.

Reference

Nikolsko-Rzhevskyy, A., Papell, D. H. and Prodan, R. (2014) Deviations from rules-based policy and their effects. *Journal of Economic Dynamics and Control* 49(December): 4–17.

ABOUT THE IEA

The Institute is a research and educational charity (No. CC 235 351), limited by guarantee. Its mission is to improve understanding of the fundamental institutions of a free society by analysing and expounding the role of markets in solving economic and social problems.

The IEA achieves its mission by:

- a high-quality publishing programme
- conferences, seminars, lectures and other events
- outreach to school and college students
- brokering media introductions and appearances

The IEA, which was established in 1955 by the late Sir Antony Fisher, is an educational charity, not a political organisation. It is independent of any political party or group and does not carry on activities intended to affect support for any political party or candidate in any election or referendum, or at any other time. It is financed by sales of publications, conference fees and voluntary donations.

In addition to its main series of publications the IEA also publishes three issues a year of a double-blind refereed academic journal, *Economic Affairs*.

The IEA is aided in its work by a distinguished international Academic Advisory Council and an eminent panel of Honorary Fellows. Together with other academics, they review prospective IEA publications, their comments being passed on anonymously to authors. All IEA papers are therefore subject to the same rigorous independent refereeing process as used by leading academic journals.

IEA publications enjoy widespread classroom use and course adoptions in schools and universities. They are also sold throughout the world and often translated/reprinted.

Since 1974 the IEA has helped to create a worldwide network of 100 similar institutions in over 70 countries. They are all independent but share the IEA's mission.

Views expressed in the IEA's publications are those of the authors, not those of the Institute (which has no corporate view), its Managing Trustees, Academic Advisory Council members or senior staff.

Members of the Institute's Academic Advisory Council, Honorary Fellows, Trustees and Staff are listed on the following page.

The Institute gratefully acknowledges financial support for its publications programme and other work from a generous benefaction by the late Professor Ronald Coase.

Other books recently published by the IEA include:

… and the Pursuit of Happiness – Wellbeing and the Role of Government
Edited by Philip Booth
Readings 64; ISBN 978-0-255-36656-4; £12.50

Public Choice – A Primer
Eamonn Butler
Occasional Paper 147; ISBN 978-0-255-36650-2; £10.00

The Profit Motive in Education – Continuing the Revolution
Edited by James B. Stanfield
Readings 65; ISBN 978-0-255-36646-5; £12.50

Which Road Ahead – Government or Market?
Oliver Knipping & Richard Wellings
Hobart Paper 171; ISBN 978-0-255-36619-9; £10.00

The Future of the Commons – Beyond Market Failure and Government Regulation
Elinor Ostrom et al.
Occasional Paper 148; ISBN 978-0-255-36653-3; £10.00

Redefining the Poverty Debate – Why a War on Markets Is No Substitute for a War on Poverty
Kristian Niemietz
Research Monograph 67; ISBN 978-0-255-36652-6; £12.50

The Euro – the Beginning, the Middle … and the End?
Edited by Philip Booth
Hobart Paperback 39; ISBN 978-0-255-36680-9; £12.50

The Shadow Economy
Friedrich Schneider & Colin C. Williams
Hobart Paper 172; ISBN 978-0-255-36674-8; £12.50

Quack Policy – Abusing Science in the Cause of Paternalism
Jamie Whyte
Hobart Paper 173; ISBN 978-0-255-36673-1; £10.00

Foundations of a Free Society
Eamonn Butler
Occasional Paper 149; ISBN 978-0-255-36687-8; £12.50

The Government Debt Iceberg
Jagadeesh Gokhale
Research Monograph 68; ISBN 978-0-255-36666-3; £10.00

A U-Turn on the Road to Serfdom
Grover Norquist
Occasional Paper 150; ISBN 978-0-255-36686-1; £10.00

New Private Monies – A Bit-Part Player?
Kevin Dowd
Hobart Paper 174; ISBN 978-0-255-36694-6; £10.00

From Crisis to Confidence – Macroeconomics after the Crash
Roger Koppl
Hobart Paper 175; ISBN 978-0-255-36693-9; £12.50

Advertising in a Free Society
Ralph Harris and Arthur Seldon
With an introduction by Christopher Snowdon
Hobart Paper 176; ISBN 978-0-255-36696-0; £12.50

Selfishness, Greed and Capitalism: Debunking Myths about the Free Market
Christopher Snowdon
Hobart Paper 177; ISBN 978-0-255-36677-9; £12.50

Waging the War of Ideas
John Blundell
Occasional Paper 131; ISBN 978-0-255-36684-7; £12.50

Brexit: Directions for Britain Outside the EU
Ralph Buckle, Tim Hewish, John C. Hulsman, Iain Mansfield and Robert Oulds
Hobart Paperback 178; ISBN 978-0-255-36681-6; £12.50

Flaws and Ceilings – Price Controls and the Damage They Cause
Edited by Christopher Coyne and Rachel Coyne
Hobart Paperback 179; ISBN 978-0-255-36701-1; £12.50

Scandinavian Unexceptionalism: Culture, Markets and the Failure of Third-Way Socialism
Nima Sanandaji
Readings in Political Economy 1; ISBN 978-0-255-36704-2; £10.00

Classical Liberalism – A Primer
Eamonn Butler
Readings in Political Economy 2; ISBN 978-0-255-36707-3; £10.00

Federal Britain: The Case for Decentralisation
Philip Booth
Readings in Political Economy 3; ISBN 978-0-255-36713-4; £10.00

Forever Contemporary: The Economics of Ronald Coase
Edited by Cento Veljanovski
Readings in Political Economy 4; ISBN 978-0-255-36710-3; £15.00

Power Cut? How the EU Is Pulling the Plug on Electricity Markets
Carlo Stagnaro
Hobart Paperback 180; ISBN 978-0-255-36716-5; £10.00

Other IEA publications

Comprehensive information on other publications and the wider work of the IEA can be found at www.iea.org.uk. To order any publication please see below.

Personal customers

Orders from personal customers should be directed to the IEA:

Clare Rusbridge
IEA
2 Lord North Street
FREEPOST LON10168
London SW1P 3YZ
Tel: 020 7799 8907. Fax: 020 7799 2137
Email: sales@iea.org.uk

Trade customers

All orders from the book trade should be directed to the IEA's distributor:

NBN International (IEA Orders)
Orders Dept.
NBN International
10 Thornbury Road
Plymouth PL6 7PP
Tel: 01752 202301, Fax: 01752 202333
Email: orders@nbninternational.com

IEA subscriptions

The IEA also offers a subscription service to its publications. For a single annual payment (currently £42.00 in the UK), subscribers receive every monograph the IEA publishes. For more information please contact:

Clare Rusbridge
Subscriptions
IEA
2 Lord North Street
FREEPOST LON10168
London SW1P 3YZ
Tel: 020 7799 8907, Fax: 020 7799 2137
Email: crusbridge@iea.org.uk